P9-EGK-850

When a School Crisis Occurs

What Parents and Stakeholders Want to Know

Helen M. Sharp

ROWMAN & LITTLEFIELD EDUCATION
Lanham • New York • Toronto • Oxford

Published in the United States of America
by Rowman & Littlefield Education
A Division of Rowman & Littlefield Publishers, Inc.
A wholly owned subsidiary of The Rowman & Littlefield Publishing Group, Inc.
4501 Forbes Boulevard, Suite 200, Lanham, Maryland 20706
www.rowmaneducation.com

PO Box 317
Oxford
OX2 9RU, UK

Copyright © 2006 by Helen M. Sharp

All rights reserved. No part of this publication may be reproduced,
stored in a retrieval system, or transmitted in any form or by any
means, electronic, mechanical, photocopying, recording, or otherwise,
without the prior permission of the publisher.

British Library Cataloguing in Publication Information Available

Library of Congress Cataloging-in-Publication Data
Sharp, Helen M.
    When a school crisis occurs : what parents and stakeholders want
to know / Helen M. Sharp.
        p. cm.
    Includes bibliographical references and index.
    ISBN-13: 978-1-57886-419-5 (cloth : alk. paper)
    ISBN-10: 1-57886-419-4 (cloth : alk. paper)
    ISBN-13: 978-1-57886-420-1 (pbk. : alk. paper)
    ISBN-10: 1-57886-420-8 (pbk. : alk. paper)
    1. School crisis management—United States.   I. Title.
    LB2866.5.S48 2006
    363.11'9371—dc22   2005037175

∞™ The paper used in this publication meets the minimum requirements of
American National Standard for Information Sciences—Permanence of
Paper for Printed Library Materials, ANSI/NISO Z39.48-1992.
Manufactured in the United States of America.

Contents

Introduction

The New Imperative for School Leaders: Respond to School Stakeholders after Crisis Events

When a School Crisis Occurs . . . provides school leaders with examples of crisis correspondence and responses directed to parents and stakeholders.

Consider the nature of a school's crisis event: it is usually unexpected and serious, within or outside the school building, and often causes deep emotions to surface among members of the school community. Whether directly involved or not, school personnel and students assimilate the crisis in their own time frame, as do others outside school when they hear about what has happened.

Administrators and security personnel implement planned responses, as appropriate. However, a crisis event or situation may interrupt as well as disrupt the routine educational efforts of the school community. The crisis may threaten one's actual or perceived safety or well-being or emotional equilibrium. Often, those who respond to a crisis event may experience a temporary inability to think or respond adequately to a task at hand, until internal processing of the crisis event takes place.

If you will, recall the impact you felt and observed in others as news about the World Trade Center attacks occurred on September 11, 2001. Numbness, horror, and a sudden suspension of the task at hand were common among groups of people watching the events unfold. With the twin towers engulfed in smoke as media specialists described and analyzed the tragedy and its aftermath, television viewers found it difficult to speak.

A school administrator reacts to a crisis, initiates the school's safety plan as called for, manages an event's containment, monitors continuously, maintains contact with designated supervisors in various areas of the building and/or campus, and handles specific problems and concerns as they arise. An immediate response usually occurs expeditiously and efficiently.

After a school crisis, we need to allay the concerns of those inside the building. Our audience outside the school setting, parents and stakeholders, also need explanations, a review of the crisis, the response, and any follow-up. Parents and stakeholders are often a school's best supporters. If there is a need for discussion or input, the school leader may offer such opportunities in the correspondence.

Responding after a crisis is especially important to strengthen the existing school-home bond. Following a crisis, administrators may gather staff and students for a review of the event. Or, individual classes or grade-level meetings may precede resumption of the usual daily schedule. School staff may aid closure via this review, in turn helping to restore building order and routine. Fears and concerns are put to rest with questions answered and one's experience shared with others.

As a school leader, you need not review a whole response scenario with either parents or stakeholders unless you deem it essential. Moreover, you need not give away secure information.

There may be a significant problem, however. A school leader in the throes of a crisis event may not have the time or the emotional distance to respond, vent, or allow emotions to surface and be dealt with, especially when containment and safety issues remain. The process of containing and responding to a crisis may overshadow the leader's personal reactions and concerns. Then assessment and review take precedence—meeting with the safety team, consulting perhaps with police in order to debrief, and listening to suggestions offered by support personnel such as counselors who specialize in crisis response. And still the need to respond to parents and stakeholders remains.

When a School Crisis Occurs . . . offers school leaders illustrative, purposeful correspondence to be used after containment of a school's crisis event. You may have already experienced unexpected school crises to which you responded with appropriate action for resolution and safety. And if you think back to one or more of these experiences, you realize you could not necessarily plan and write your most effective response on the day of the event or even soon thereafter.

Hopefully, your school(s) will not be the setting for any of the crisis situations that comprise the bulk of this book. However, you can utilize the models provided in *When a School Crisis Occurs* . . . if a crisis does occur. The models provide you with a prompt, a start for your timely response/follow-up. You may feel pressured to respond quickly even when a situation leaves you drained. You will undoubtedly want to personalize individual letters and describe as much as you consider appropriate for readers. But you will have a starting point.

CONSIDER SCHOOL STAKEHOLDERS

When a school crisis occurs, do you have a choice about responding to those outside the school setting? *Stakeholders* are individuals or groups who are usually members of your community, as you already know. Besides parents, stakeholders include an individual school's immediate neighbors, the community's business and civic leaders, its realtors and media representatives, and the faculty and staff of the local community college or a nearby university, for example. Many individuals in these groups maintain an interest in the local schools and the school district, including the operations, policies, and procedures that govern daily learning activities and programs.

When a school crisis occurs, stakeholders want to know the details about the specific incident or event, and that the problem was handled or resolved promptly and in a satisfactory manner.

What sources of school information do your stakeholders rely on? Can you utilize the next district newsletter to review a crisis? Many newsletters appear only quarterly, though they are a very good source of pertinent information. There are other possibilities, especially the local or community newspaper, which might run an administrator's open Letter to the Editor or a feature story/interview in which the school leader(s) can explain a crisis. An administrator's monthly column is also a good source of information. Announcements or bulletins with explanations for local television and/or radio stations are also sources to convey school news, and newspeople almost always follow up an initial story with successive updates.

There is everything to gain from a steady output of information that goes to members of the community, especially since almost all students, faculty and staff members, besides relevant events and activities of the school, are of interest to so many people. Stakeholders cannot feel they know the school or the district's events without information coming from inside the buildings.

Many would argue you do not need a public relations specialist when a school crisis occurs because the more personal explanation provided by a school administrator is preferable. The tone and style of an administrator's messages reflect a less formal approach than a media specialist's; an administrator cannot help but gain the interest and support of readers when that administrator takes the time to inform, reassure, and invite input or readers' expertise, as appropriate. Readers become more familiar with the administrator's priorities and with the person behind the title, as well as obtain a full treatment of an important topic.

Stakeholders want to know an orderly academic routine is in process, with students engaged in learning activities, as soon as the crisis is handled. Who better than school leaders can write the necessary message?

Chapter One

The Decision to Respond at Another Time or Not to Respond

What happens when follow-up after a school crisis does not occur? Let me provide an example.

In a high-school setting, the race for the senior-class presidency brought two outstanding young men to everyone's attention. One of the candidates, raised in Southeast Asia, had escaped his country with his parents.

Both students' campaigns and speeches to elicit student body support were well-received, but what followed was the Southeast Asian student's dismay and then deep hurt: on the morning of the election, someone had written in bold black marker on each of his posters *Remember the war in Vietnam. Vote for*_____ (the opposing student candidate's name).

As a result, an unknown administrator was rumored to have awarded the presidency to the student of Southeast-Asian descent. The announcement of the new student leader was simple enough, but no school meetings, no explanation from administrators followed. Students and faculty members talked among themselves, agreeing that student discussion groups with faculty moderators might have been appropriate. Because the final decision was suddenly out of their hands, students seemed uneasy with *the school's* decision: this was an appointment, not their election, as they had expected. Who knows how students might have voted? The election was supposed to be the choice of a majority of the students.

The school year proceeded, but the hasty resolution of the election issue remained on the minds of students, faculty, and staff members.

What about the questions students, parents, and stakeholders might have raised? What had occurred, followed by awarding the position to one of the candidates, called for an explanation from an administrator.

In contrast, a follow-up after a crisis incident, especially in writing, allows all who have been involved in or witnessed or heard about the crisis to receive and, perhaps, offer opportunities for feedback. Follow-up may help closure occur for students, parents, and stakeholders. An administrator, when mindful of the new imperative, starts the resumption of normal school processes and restores order by corresponding with parents and stakeholders as well as by offering students opportunities to talk about and deal with unusual and unsettling circumstances.

Chapter Two

Consider a
District Communication Policy

Does your district need a statement that emphasizes the importance of communication between school personnel and stakeholders outside of school? Consider the following:

All adults in an educational community represent the school district on paper and in e-mail transmissions. Creating the best possible impression goes a long way in terms of maintaining a school's credibility and that of the district. All communication efforts offer the opportunity to tell those outside the buildings that the school and district are doing well. You can hardly overlook opportunities to respond: school districts need good publicity, the kind that comes as a result of gifted, committed educators doing their best to lead and/or teach students as well as to handle crisis situations.

The faculty handbook might well include a statement explaining the importance of each letter, bulletin, report, and news brief sent from administrators, faculty, and staff members to parents, school stakeholders, and the media. Contrast a verbal statement announced in a staff meeting with a written message: though pointed and well explained, verbal messages may soon be forgotten after the meeting or discussions conclude. In written form, the statement about effective communications becomes a priority item, a standard important enough to be included in a guide or bulletin to inform staff members about administrators' expectations.

A SAMPLE COMMUNICATION POLICY (PURPOSE: TO SET THE DESIRED STANDARD, AS ILLUSTRATED BELOW)

Gibson School District No. 8 board members and administrators prioritize and encourage clear, effective, purposeful, and correct communication in all written and oral messages to parents, stakeholders, and the media [identify the school district in the first sentence].

All effective messages originating from administrators, faculty, and staff reflect a concise style, cordial tone, and an understandable, meaningful message. District personnel also emphasize sensitivity to the needs, interests, and possible questions of the multicultural student population, if applicable, and the surrounding community, especially since all readers seek specific information and explanations. Explaining to and informing readers becomes a critical link to our public outside the school buildings, especially after a crisis situation. Clear explanations and examples help readers understand. One other important suggestion may be evident but worth repetition: Anticipate your readers' questions and concerns, asking yourself, "What do readers want or need to know about this issue or topic?"

Reports, letters, and progress evaluations sent home as well as newsletters, media fact sheets, and publicity briefs, summaries of policies and the effects thereof, and informal mailings seeking, for example, support of an election issue, should convey a district's purpose and commitment to offer each student meaningful, challenging, and purposeful educational experiences. We continue to strengthen in this way the school district's commitment and purpose, its tradition of excellence in every aspect of students' learning and the school environment. Each of us represents District No. 8 in all of our communications.

Our goal is to create the most meaningful learning experience for students. Of course, always include specifics about how and when the recipient of the message may contact the writer if questions or further explanations warrant follow-up.

Chapter Three

Essential Writing Terms, and Suggestions for Writing Successful, Efficient Messages

Writing Terms

Purpose

Why are you writing this message? Purposes: to inform or explain, to persuade, to reassure, to offer understanding or sympathy. The message might well have several purposes. Write out your purpose statement before you begin writing a document. You thereby direct your writing.

Audience

The receiver is the audience, an interested audience. Anticipate what the audience members' concerns and questions might be; crisis documents call for a serious tone, a businesslike and authoritative stance.
Audience: parents, students, community members, board members, teachers or staff (perhaps a number of these or all of these).
Carefully reread the document when completed or give it to someone else to read, with the question "Does this sound appropriate for parents?" For example, one enterprising young teacher started a student progress report with "This is a follow-up to the forgery incident." Whatever response he expected, the teacher-writer neglected to anticipate the parents' potential dissatisfaction or anger when he brought up a negative incident from the past. Something more hopeful would gain compliance, such as "Jerome has a perfect homework record for the past month; I am pleased with his progress." What might follow could

involve suggestions for improvement in class attention and behavior, for example.

Tone   The attitude of the writer. A neutral, objective tone giving factual information is always correct. A neutral tone
or businesslike tone also leaves out the writer's emotion.
Angry or curt responses or those that accuse or seem
to demand compliance rarely succeed in their purpose; instead, readers respond with irritation or anger.
Always avoid a harsh or angry tone. Write at another
time if your own emotions are negative, for the emotions will surface as you write.

Style   Straightforward, shorter rather than longer. Does the
situation call for your own objectivity? This means
the writer is apparently uninvolved one way or the
other; the message is primarily factual, explanatory.
Some sample correspondences in this book will show
an involved writer, as appropriate for the situation.

Opener   Get right to the point, identifying in the initial sentences the subject of the letter and your purpose.

Document Length   1½ pages, double-spaced

Sentence Length   Ten to thirteen words per sentence tend to convey
meaning better than long sentences (the exception
might be scholarly and research writing).

Paragraphing   A single-sentence paragraph is perfectly appropriate;
a paragraph of no more than three typed lines looks
easy to read and is more likely to be read. A paragraph
containing one idea is also more likely to be easily
understood.
In almost all cases, readers prefer single-thought paragraphs.

Suggestions for Effective Writing

Truth   Tell the truth if you decide it would be better than allowing rumors to circulate—or indicate clearly that
the matter has legal implications, for example, requiring careful handling, and that you cannot comment or
put details about the matter into print at this time.

The truth always comes out, sooner or later, as you know.

Emphasis

Above all, call attention to the safety and well-being of students and their supervision by adults. We must account for each and every student all day long. That is our number one concern, always.

Revision

Rereading and revising waste time just when you need to get a message out quickly—don't you agree? But hold on a minute. Reread the correspondence several times and revise, despite your timeline. Plus, allow one or two others who are good proofreader-spellers to read and offer suggestions about any changes that might be necessary—even changes you might have overlooked.

Remember, the message must be error-free, well-worded, and easily understood; you attain those qualities through revision/rewriting. Stunning, perfect messages rarely result from a single written effort. Writers revise—a lot.

When Ernest Hemingway wrote a story or novel, he started his daily writing by rereading, correcting, and changing what he had already written. The result is a clipped, clean, measured, and businesslike effect; his was a spare, polished, but pointed style. That comes from revising.

Emotional Impact(s)

As you reread a post-crisis message, consider the range of emotions possible for a reader. Might readers experience apprehension about their child's safety? Annoyance due to a sudden change in academic requirements? Frustration with the lack of communication between the school and home? Anger, for example, related to necessary remediation or additional one-on-one work between teacher and student, which has not caused a student's improvement? Consider the readers' emotions as you write the message. Always keep your readers in mind.

Demanding or
High-Handed Parents

No one accepts criticism, hostility, or second-guessing easily. Instead, focus reader attention on facts, facts, and more facts. Proof-positive facts. And specifics.

Carefully documented facts and specifics prove your point and counter the few parents who voice strong criticisms of you or who try to intimidate you. Keep repeating the facts, such as school policy, specific rules and procedures, expectations of students, district and course goals, and benchmarks, as well as various test grades, homework assignments completed, participation, in-class behavior, attitude, and so forth.

A School's Goal   To provide the best educational opportunities for students day-by-day: repeat this in any way you wish; just repeat it often to parents.

[Additional note: A series of examples related to the above follows, but skip these if you need no further illustrations.]

Chapter Four

Illustrations of Terms and Suggestions

The crisis: The death of a former basketball coach and one of this school's strongest supporters, Coach Bud Weaver

Purpose

To inform staff and students about Weaver's death, plus services that will follow.

Audience

Adults and students, parents and stakeholders (everyone in the South Suburban League area who knew or knew about Coach Weaver).

Anticipating the audience's questions: Readers want to know what caused the coach's death, whether he had a history of heart disease, for example, and if he was taking care of himself in spite of his schedule of activities and the assistant coaching responsibilities he had assumed. Readers also want to know if there is anything they can do for Bud Weaver's family members, as individuals or as a group. Also, they may wonder about collecting funds for his favorite charity. Many will wonder who will carry on the Weaver tradition.

Tone

Emotional, serious, sad and heartfelt, respectful.

An example excerpt from the school office announcement: Our *beloved* Coach Weaver, *spirited* backer of all Central High School athletic teams since 1986, died suddenly at his lakeside home this morning. [Note: the emotion is in the italicized words; the message and topic is serious.]

9

Style   Straightforward, factual example of special announce-
                      ment, with facts specified: Coach Bud Weaver suffered a
                      sudden fatal heart attack last night [fact] despite primary-
                      care physician Dr. Bryan Dalton's assessment that he
                      knew Bud was in excellent physical condition [fact]. Dr.
                      Dalton said, "Bud was really anticipating our season
                      schedule flyers coming out on time [fact]; he supervised
                      the writing and printing [fact]. He also helped all of our
                      coaches during practices and planned to continue. He
                      loved sports and had always offered his expertise [facts].
                      I had no indication Bud was experiencing health prob-
                      lems in any way [fact]."

Opener   "I know you will join me in a schoolwide, three-minute pe-
                      riod of silence tomorrow as we start the day and remember
                      Coach Bud Weaver." [This is Principal Paul Handler's spe-
                      cial bulletin to all faculty and staff members.]

Length   Four paragraphs, as planned below:
                      Paragraph 1: Facts about Weaver's personality and char-
                      acter, career highlights, past responsibilities, and out-
                      standing successes
                      Paragraph 2: Quotes from the board president, current
                      superintendent, and current coaches as they reflect on
                      Weaver's contributions and his involvement with all the
                      school's athletes and their successes as well as his con-
                      cern for all students.
                      Paragraph 3: Arrangements for a memorial gathering to
                      recollect and celebrate Weaver's life and philosophy; also
                      time and place for visitation at funeral home; day, time
                      of funeral.
                      Paragraph 4: A call for written memorials of Coach
                      Weaver to be given in a memory book collection to Mrs.
                      Weaver, and the appropriate forms to use: letters, anec-
                      dotes, essays covering what you want to remember about
                      Coach (i.e., stories he used to teach students on and off
                      the field), your favorite episode involving Coach, humor-
                      ous or otherwise. We are asking for as many as possible.

Sentence Length   Various lengths: short, dramatic sentences may portray
                      strong emotions; long, detailed sentences can offer expla-
                      nations and details.

Style

Straightforward, as these sentences illustrate: Let's not forget Coach Bud Weaver. What do you think is a good way to remember him in a very special way? I will chair the committee to establish some type of campus or building plaque or memorial for Coach. Let's all consider this project: Please give me your suggestions for a permanent memorial. I'll read them all. This was Bud's school, as much as yours or mine.

Chapter Five

Appropriate School Apparel

The crisis: Students have begun to wear almost anything they choose to school. Some have displayed gang affiliations on shirts; others seem dressed for a day at the beach or an evening at a nightclub. Students' and parents' compliance with appropriate standards of dress befitting orderly instructional activities is sought.

The high school's policy committee recommends setting guidelines for student apparel, and board members encourage follow-up. The principal responds.

Dear Parents/Guardians and Students,

I look forward to meeting all parents/guardians during our first open house of the school year, in just three short weeks. Getting your sons and daughters off to a strong start is our first priority [cordial opening, positive tone, engages reader for compliance].

Our board members, faculty, and staff submitted suggestions to the policy committee recommending appropriate student wearing apparel, a dress code for Clearview High School District 109. Individual committee members suggested that a year or two's trial run with a dress code might be accepted more readily than a requirement for all students to wear khaki trousers and their choice of three colors of polo shirts (white, navy, black), as some schools had opted. Discussions about student apparel occurred during all three of our summer meetings. I want to share some of the specifics of the revised rules, which are listed in the student handbook [letter's purpose].

Instead of mandating the khakis and polo shirts, committee members felt students would respond favorably to these rules; hopefully, all parents/guardians will agree. We expect students to use good judgment in choosing school attire appropriate for learning. School is a preparation for further academic study but also for work settings later on. Although dress codes have relaxed somewhat in both school and business arenas, we want to restate our expectations—until our students are out of school and on their own [expectations of students assuming responsibility for their wearing appropriate dress to school].

The requirement for appropriate apparel was written to suggest the preference for comfortable but more formal dress for school, not to be confused with torn, dirty, revealing, provocative, distracting or offensive items [specific items will be noted in succeeding paragraphs].

Male students are asked to avoid overly large, baggy, or loose trousers. Besides their usual identification as specific groups' apparel, this style of trousers interferes with walking and causes embarrassment if the pants fall down. Last year this did occur. An upperclassman tried to ignore or laugh-off the teasing and comments the rest of the year, but it was difficult. He was known as "the Senior with the Pants Problem." Also, male students should not roll up their trouser legs.

Hoodies or other garments with potentially offensive drawings, slogans, writings, or excerpts from other documents and the like are not acceptable; if the student has any doubts, the student should ask his or her parents/guardians or check with a faculty or staff member before wearing the garment. The insignia of specific groups is also not acceptable on any garment, T-shirts included (the exception is our school-logo T-shirts).

In essence: Drawings, slogans, and other writings are unacceptable on clothing worn by males or females in our school district, with the only exception noted above, our school-logo T-shirts.

Also, students should avoid wearing shorts altogether, and should choose long pants instead. We maintain controlled-temperature rooms, guaranteeing students' comfort year-round.

Flip-flops, though popular, are also nonregulation items; they cause difficulty walking up and down stairs because they are more cumbersome than regular shoes. In carpeted areas of the building it is too easy for anyone to stumble and trip wearing flip-flops. For safety's sake, and knowing that all of us sometimes rush to our next class and that flip-flops do not give us the control we need, we must ask students to refrain from wearing these. Also, students should tie their shoelaces; it is very easy to lose untied high-tops, for example, while walking [explanations with requirement].

Students might plan ahead for the next day, setting out their apparel choice(s) after considering all the best options and their activities the next day [plan to accommodate the policy].

Students should not wear bandanas or otherwise display them as part of their attire [specific detail].

As noted in the handbook, we will follow up all concerns about clothing. Please be advised that if a student is written up or reportedly not wearing clothing deemed appropriate, he/she must call his/her parents and arrange a ride home to change to acceptable clothing and obtain a ride back as soon as possible. Inside suspension(s) will also be assigned as appropriate [statement of penalties for violation of dress code].

Young women have similar obligations; thus, we do not expect to see any provocative clothing. This includes low-cut or tight, revealing blouses or T-shirts, tank or tube tops, or gauze/lace garments. We do not expect to see any garment that bares the midriff. Skirts or dresses cannot be more than two inches above the knee. Peasant-style long skirts are likely to get in the way as the student walks; although not specifically prohibited, students should avoid wearing these. Female students have had problems on stairways with these long garments, which restrict movement. Halter-style dresses or halter blouses are similarly inappropriate. Thin, spaghetti-style straps on any garment indicate an inappropriate choice of apparel—unacceptable because they are out of place in our academic environment.

Distressed or faded jeans and jackets are acceptable if not torn, stained, or showing holes in the material.

Shoes must fit; running/training shoes should be securely tied. Again, students should avoid wearing flip-flops. If our young women choose to wear anklestrap-style shoes or thin dancers' shoes and then take them off when the shoes become uncomfortable, they must make sure to have a second pair available for the rest of the day. No one should be barefoot in our building. Or, students should take the time out of the school day for their parents/guardians to transport them to and from school [consequences follow non-regulation footwear].

I have explained these few guidelines about acceptable and inappropriate school attire. Mrs. Sampson in Guidance supplied some of the details. Either of us would be happy to talk with parents/guardians or students individually, of course.

Students should also be cautious about what *day* they might choose to wear clothing of questionable appropriateness. If a student is written up for a clothing violation and it is a test day in any class, the student may well expect a makeup test if he/she misses a class. This may not be the same test other students completed [consequences following student choices].

We appreciate your cooperation and understanding.

Please call the office with your questions and/or comments; I will get back to you as soon as possible.

Sincerely,

Chapter Six

Principal's Letter to Stakeholders

The following letter to the editor appeared in the local newspaper:

Dear Neighbors in the Wildwood Elementary School area,

I appreciate receiving your e-mails, letters, and phone calls regarding parents transporting our students to and from Wildwood. Without your feedback, I would not know that a problem exists, especially since most of our students ride the buses both to and from Wildwood [cordial tone; writer appreciates feedback].

Thankfully, our local police officers continue to help us monitor the vehicular traffic around our school exits, with the primary goal of efficient boarding of buses. Officers are aware of the parents' waiting/parking problems.

We do not experience difficulties in the morning, but do after school. Let me state the problem as clearly as I can: Parents or relatives who arrive to pick up children after school should not park in residents' driveways, on the shoulder areas at the edge of lawns, or on the streets around the school. Parents will argue "It's just a few minutes," but our officers assure us they will soon ticket cars, whether the car engines are running or shut off.

If parents or relatives arrive early to pick up children (and they usually do so), we suggest that you homeowners make the first contact, speaking to the drivers who park in front of your home or in your driveway. A courteous reminder from you that you do not want drivers parking in your driveway or on the edge of your lawn may also be followed by your approaching police officers if drivers fail to comply. Write down the car license number and description, of course, and the times and dates of improper parking occasions. Obstructing traffic or interfering with buses entering and exiting the school are serious matters. Parents are advised never to park anywhere except in the

15

back of the school, in the parking lot [first approach: individual homeowners speak to drivers; penalty ticket may follow].

Officers in charge of our building traffic advise us that because of the number of buses and cars that utilize these roadways, they want Greenwood Avenue and Boole Street clear at all times, and free of parked cars, to keep the traffic moving [a police order to keep two major roads clear at all times might emphasize your request to drivers].

Parents were advised via initial bulletins sent home not to park on these two busy roadways or in neighbors' driveways.

We have designed the school's driveway circle arrangement for students waiting for a parent to pick them up. Ideally, students move rapidly—and they usually do—from their place in line to the monitor assigned to help them get into their car and onto the circle path out of the driveway.

Officers have advised us that they prefer parents parking their cars in back of the school, getting out of the car, and then accompanying their child from the line of students waiting and walking back to the lot.

I welcome additional comments and suggestions, however. If you as a property owner are not satisfied or if our requests are not complied with around your home, let's talk. The best time to call me is after school, usually 3:30 daily, except Wednesday, faculty meeting time [open line of communication for feedback].

Sincerely,

Chapter Seven

School Building Safety

Advance Preparation for Potential Crisis Events: An Explanation

As you know, each and every student must be accounted for at all times. Attendance/roll-taking occurs so that the school office staff knows where each student is located throughout the school day, emergency or not.

Parents may want to pick their children up when the threat of an emergency occurs. Explain your special-circumstance attendance plan, informing parents about the plan that will allow them to arrive at school and pick up their child at their convenience. Parents expect this.

Do parents know the terms *lockdown* and *evacuation* as you use them in school-crisis situations?

Are parents aware of your crisis-response team or the group of community members who meet at school to aid administrators and the school safety team in the event of emergency circumstances? Supervising students at all times is a priority for all educators; repeat this obligation for students.

However, unusual weather conditions may occur suddenly. Road conditions change rapidly during winter weather, for example, in many areas of the country. Heavy traffic on major roads compromise safety when there is the threat of a storm or other unusual weather conditions. Will your school buses use other routes to transport students if evacuation is indicated?

School leaders who share selective information about crisis and emergency procedures before the emergencies occur gain compliance of parents whose concern for their children's well-being may cause them to be demanding and/or frantic in an emergency. How do you prepare school faculty and staff to respond to demanding, frantic parents? Might selected school personnel, including instructors, receive the list of locations each class is assigned to in an emergency? Do faculty and staff members need to know the emergency bus locations?

Not utilizing all those who can help in potential emergencies and/or unusual or threatening conditions and circumstances—for example, safety teams within each building; police department personnel; traffic experts; community crisis responders ready and available on short notice; local weather buffs; ham radio services and local news and television and radio channels—may compromise your school safety plan. Each school location is different from all others, demanding a unique response to weather emergencies or the need to evacuate a school building and the use of appropriate road access and circumstances specific to the surrounding area; i.e., heavy traffic on major roads as buses exit their school stations.

As a school leader, you can create new teams and committees to assess conditions and confer with experts; you may want to utilize university personnel who have studied and researched the area in which you are located, in addition to crisis-response experts, to assess and plan for successful responses from all students and school personnel within the buildings. Drills and practices, plus explanations, allow students to know and be prepared to follow the specific procedures in response to an emergency.

Chapter Eight

Sample Letter from Administrator to Parents about School Safety

Dear Parents/Guardians,

In Elanville School District, our number one priority is the safety and security of all students and staff members during the school day and in after-school events and activities. Your child might refer to various school safety practices and ask you questions, and this letter reviews some of our procedures.

District safety teams may utilize lockdown or evacuation of our buildings in situations that might compromise safety and security during the school day. For your information, the safety teams and select members of our security staff also routinely attend home and away athletic events.

Lockdown

Building lockdowns are responses to internal threats; for example, a student might have a knife or weapon with him; an outsider may gain entry to our schools; an altercation between students or several groups of students might occur. In these cases, the school security team and its director advise our administrators to keep students in the classes to which they are assigned. Attendance is taken on Special Attendance Report forms and picked up and entered into a database by staff members in order that we may account for each district student in these circumstances.

Evacuation

Evacuation of any and all school buildings may occur when an internal or external threat seems unpredictable or poses danger. We might evacuate when there is a noxious odor present, a fire of any type, or the threat of a potential incendiary device detonating inside the building.

Our security staff and safety team, including community crisis team members who have received training or possess expertise in such threats, assemble on site, receiving an overview/briefing, from our building specialists. The group then assesses the threat and recommends a specific course of action or containment of the threat.

Students may temporarily leave the building with the classroom teacher who utilizes the attendance report forms mentioned above to account for each student. School personnel have been assigned to compile the attendance rolls, again assuring our knowledge of where all students are temporarily located, accompanied by classroom instructors and additional school staff members. Specific sites have been recommended by safety experts and local police in case of emergencies and are known by staff and instructors; these locations are indicated in the school safety response plans we utilize internally.

In these exit events, each wing of the school will assemble, with all classes led by instructors if an evacuation is indicated.

We may also dismiss students to buses; the handbook lists the temporary **emergency locations** of all bus routes so that students may board their usual buses.

Unusual Building or Weather Conditions

Circumstances that compromise teaching and learning may occur during the day unrelated to the threats mentioned previously. The loss of heating or air conditioning, severe weather alerts, weather conditions suggesting a natural disaster is imminent or possible (mudslides, flooding, unusually high wind gusts, a tornado or hurricane). All of these may cause a city Weather Watch 5 alert, suggesting temporary school evacuation or early dismissal.

Our administrators alert *Channel 5 TV News* of our decisions in these events. Decisions are also carried on Clear Radio 108.5. SafetyServe Bus Company assures us all routes served will assemble within 20–30 minutes for student pickup.

Major Roads with Heavy Traffic in Emergencies

One problem, which has not occurred but might in the future, is a weather problem or related circumstance calling for school dismissal. However, the weather or related circumstance might also affect other area schools as well as businesses and industries. City and regional transportation management representatives reveal that excessive traffic could easily clog heavily utilized highways and major roads in our vicinity. A standstill might well result.

The answer to such road jams in their view is assigning each section of our tri-county area to use only certain specified roads in the event of emergencies. They realize a plan of this type will allow timelier exiting and movement onward toward a destination. The experts are assessing how this might serve all users more efficiently if everyone complied. All school leaders and businesses anticipate their report and recommendations. I will update you as decisions are made and their implementation suggested.

This brief informational overview of potential building and weather emergencies provides some details to acquaint you with District 102 plans. I would be happy to meet with you if you seek additional information. We welcome feedback from any parents/guardians or specialists interested and/or trained in handling the emergencies and situations reviewed above.

Dr. Sanchez and I have regular daily office hours for your convenience in calling us. My open office hours are 1–3 p.m., daily; if I am not in my office when you call, I will get back to you as quickly as I can.

Preparation for response to internal and external events that impact our students and staff during the school day is an obligation that we take very seriously, and we will continue to do so. Let me hear about your concerns and/or suggestions as they occur.

Sincerely,

Chapter Nine

Principal's News Story (Stakeholders' Information)

Withdrawal of Upperclassmen's Open Campus Lunch Hour

The following feature appeared in the local newspaper:

Open Campus Lunch Not Working

The open campus lunch hours for upperclassmen of Big Harbor High School cease this week. School board members, faculty, and staff personnel received negative feedback about the privilege. The results were not anticipated with the trial run.

Some students elected to eat in the cafeteria and then study in Room 120 Quiet Study Hall or go to the library or computer room. Those students raved about the extra time.

Many students drove to the Coffee Cup or Grandma's Café in town. Though students were neither boisterous nor troublesome, restaurant owners said the rush of students all at once was "like a stampede" and "overwhelming." There were not enough servers to accommodate the students, in addition to regular customers from local offices and businesses.

Student tardies in sixth-hour classes increased almost 40 percent during the trial run. Many excuses seemed hard to believe ("I couldn't get the bill for ten minutes," for example). Our school population is at its highest level this year, and the trickle of late students forced attendance personnel to write entry passes to classes, slowing them down with their regular responsibilities. Some students missed fully half the sixth class period as a result.

Teachers felt obligated to start the lesson anew, accommodating the latecomers. Students were upset if they missed a quiz, feeling penalized if they could not take a makeup.

A third factor involved parking. Students took available spaces on both Ridge Avenue and Hightower Road rather than the student parking lot. They wanted to avoid the delays out of the student lot after school. A number of complaints from area residents related that Ridge and Hightower were convenient places to park and then walk to the nature center. With spaces taken, residents needed to drive and walk extra distances, and they felt this was burdensome.

At this point, there are no plans to resume the open lunch schedule, even in a modified version.

Administrative staff members and the attendance office will compile data revealing numbers of students utilizing the privilege versus those who stayed on campus; total number of complaints and concerns and types of issues reported, both from outside and inside the high school; and parents' feedback and sixth-period teachers' input.

Chapter Ten

Weather Conditions and Potential Hazards

Potential crisis: Unexpected severe weather; weather conditions

Dear Parents/Guardians,

Our district policy governing responses to weather concerns and potential hazards was the subject of scrutiny for our West Euclid District No. 24 board members and me this summer. We amended the policy in view of the emergencies last year, which were eye-openers [background for letter].

Let me review some background for you.

When Mr. Hammett and I, along with our board president, drove all our bus route roads that early morning the second week of February, I recall experiencing great difficulty with icy patches on nearly every road within our school zone and the limits of our district [key bus transportation factor: safety in view of road surfaces].

District personnel will take all weather forecasts very seriously and err on the side of safety and caution, as we have at times in the past. Our local television *Your Weather Channel 9* personnel will broadcast continuous weather warnings at the bottom of your TV screens, including our decisions to close school, as necessary. They will break into programming each hour to update viewers about inclement weather conditions [information about local television station].

We need your help as we begin school once again:

1. If you will be available to transport your child from school in the event of a weather emergency, indicate that on the enclosed (pink) card. Note both sides of the card. One side calls for a phone number where we can always reach you, and/or

2. A list of three adults who have your permission to pick up and take home your child from school. We need the names, addresses, and phone numbers of these adults.

In addition to Channel 9 bulletins, we will broadcast decisions of early dismissal in anticipation of weather-related emergencies on 90.9 WEAP.

Weather emergencies require quick responses, and your cooperation in completing these pink cards will help us prepare to clear the buildings and monitor the youths. Of course, we never know when something like this may occur, so your timely response is much appreciated [information to keep on file in school office related to each child in school].

Please plan to discuss appropriate behavior with your son or daughter should an emergency occur. They must gather belongings, obey dismissal procedures, get their coats and supplies from lockers, and remain with their attendance room teacher until notification to proceed to the buses or cars. Adult supervisors will always lead each attendance room group out of the building for pickup at designated places around the building. We will run through practice drills as often as possible until we have smooth efficiency in exiting. Students will become accustomed to the attendance check-off each and every practice run [parents must encourage good behavior].

Even if your home is within walking distance of the buildings, we prefer an adult accompany each child in the event of weather and other emergencies. Let's take all the precautions we can. Otherwise, without the pink card on file, your child will walk home despite an emergency if he or she usually walks home.

As a reminder, let me list the emergencies that have occurred in West Euclid prior to my tenure, over the past eight years: the fire in the coaches' lounge; the heating system in the elementary building suddenly quitting, during January, of course; the explosion in the paint factory on Temple Road—we are too close to Temple to take any chances, you know—and the February 1 frost they still talk about, when the air temperature suddenly dropped during a winter rain and froze on the roads. This last incident, a lulu, created what my predecessor called "the worst driving conditions imaginable, a nightmare."

We can meet any emergency if we are prepared, and prepared we will be— with your cooperation.

I am available to discuss any specific concerns you may have; afternoons are better than mornings. If you would like to help us in the event of emergencies, let us know and we will assign you to a room or committee [available for questions, concerns].

I appreciate your cooperation and feedback.

Sincerely,

[Notice the writing style of this school leader; his message is somewhat informal in its language, seeking to put readers at ease and assure them of his concern to maintain the children's safety. The touches of humor are not overdone nor are they really noticeable. This leader is up-front about everything; weather and related emergencies will not defeat him. Readers are most likely confident about his ability to handle emergencies. Your style should reflect your priorities; an informal style that sounds like you are speaking to your audience and you wish to reassure readers is preferable, say, to a neutral, strictly factual, or formal style.]

Chapter Eleven

Respect for Adults as well as for All Other Students

Potential crisis: Verbal or physical abuse of one or more students directed against another

Dear Parents/Guardians and Students,

Respect for All remains our Bayview Unified School District policy, as mandated by our board of education.

All students enrolled in our schools must be very cautious about joking and kidding for fun contrasted with verbal messages intended to hurt others, whether adults or students. Remind your sons and daughters to *think about* what they want to say before they say it.

Similarly, all students must regard any type of physical force or physical mistreatment planned or carried out against an adult or student as strictly prohibited [the preceding paragraphs are spare, specific, and clear].

Board members and I want to emphasize the no-tolerance policy in the aftermath of a recent tragedy in another district. You may be aware that a student took his own life in Seneca, just north of Hazelton. We have learned that this freshman was the victim of students throughout the school who perceived the young man was different. He had exceptional talent in the fine arts and in music, but both talents were overlooked in place of, perhaps, jealousy about the recognition he had received for his gifts.

Experts warn us that recipients of student-led punishments, verbal or physical, carry the effects with them for the rest of their lives [a consequence of abuse].

We must start each day reminding ourselves that we all possess enormous potential but that no one is better than anyone else by virtue of wealth, parents' accomplishments, home location, special talents and skills, family name or background, social status, expertise, reputation, and/or name recognition.

This is a reminder that there is no place whatsoever for any abuse of a staff member or student in Bayview USD. Similarly, there is no justification for any such behavior. Bayview staff and students face serious consequences, including potential suspension/dismissal, for any infractions of the *Respect for All* philosophy [explanation].

We are aware of trials or initiations, abusive criticism, and punishments directed against some students new to a school or new team members in some sports. Permanent suspension/dismissal will result, stemming from any infraction related to initiations or verbal abuse. We consider the use of humiliation, intimidation, threats, appropriating money, supplies, or other possessions, or expecting special favors from another student or students to fall well within the range of actions calling for immediate indefinite suspension, with dismissal pending investigation [a practice in some school districts].

In no event whatsoever is it ever acceptable to use physical force of any kind against another. No fighting. No ganging up as a group against another person or persons.

Similarly, one's race or ethnic background, sexual orientation, physical or emotional handicap, or limitation should never be addressed with lack of respect.

In addition, as mentioned, the location of harassment makes little difference if the instigators are our students. Bus drivers have reported overhearing verbal insults and have stopped their routes to call for administrators' input in the midst of such episodes. We mean no tolerance whatsoever applies, whether in class, in sports and extracurricular activities, during school days and weekends, on field trips and the like, or in activities away from Bayview [repetition underscores major point: harassment is unacceptable].

We are pleased that all our coaches will follow through with special meetings, including participants' parents, to reiterate our concerns and their experience with students' behavior and verbal exchanges.

Our tradition as a school, as a community, and as a nation stems from the single idea about treating others with equality for all, as emblazoned on our Bayview insignia.

You are welcome to contact any board member or me to explore this subject further.

Sincerely,

Chapter Twelve

Reassignment to Other Schools

A Response to Create Racial/Ethnic Balance

The crisis: A sizeable group of District 20 parents is upset about the possibility that some students comprising the current populations scheduled to attend the four district schools may be assigned to a school other than the one in their neighborhood. District 20 parents have always taken pride in their local schools.

There are four district elementary schools (Central, Ridge, Chandler, and Lincoln), but Chandler's population has a disproportionate number of nonwhite students, with the majority eligible for free and reduced-price breakfasts and lunches. Almost 8 percent of Chandler's students speak a second language. Administrators agree that balancing student populations in each of the elementary schools is a desirable goal, and the No Child Left Behind legislation fortifies their resolve.

Members of the district board of education want a lottery reassignment of students so that Central, Ridge, Chandler, and Lincoln schools all have diverse populations; three of the schools will each absorb one-quarter of Chandler's students as the appropriate number of local students relocate to another of the four schools. Federal funds are at stake and there is a priority among administrators and school staffs for apportioning school populations to reflect society at large and prepare all students for high school and beyond.

Dear Parents/Guardians,

The board of education and I share your commitment to creating and maintaining schools of excellence accommodating the needs of all our district students. Enrollment gains these last few years have called attention to school changes forthcoming. In addition, this coming year's projections indicate Chandler's population of nonwhite students will be almost 38 percent.

Our administrative team, board members, and several enrollment consultants met regularly last year to pinpoint the maximum number of students per elementary building, based on current enrollment. We also have targeted programs that will allow us to augment our enrichment opportunities and related resources. We now have an *ideal* numerical capacity for each of the four schools and a plan for balanced school enrollments, including the class sizes we want for the children—as we maintain high-quality educational opportunities for all children in the district.

We sought an objective method to assign students to our four schools and chose a lottery. You will soon receive information about this in another letter. As a result, attending the local neighborhood school will not necessarily be possible for every District 20 youth.

Let's review some of the advantages and disadvantages of the reassignment plan.

Maintaining a program of preparation for junior high and high school continues, with emphasis on appropriate mastery of academic skills and supplementary tutorials as needed. We have a strong basic skills curriculum in all four schools, which continues, keyed to our objectives. Reassignment to a new school allows some of our students a fresh start, with the opportunity to make new friends while learning in new classes from new teachers. Psychologists insist children adapt more easily to new situations than adults usually anticipate.

All students will have the opportunity to become accustomed to a diverse school population that mirrors our neighborhoods, future educational settings, and job sites. Experiencing a range of cultural, racial, and ethnic differences early in life tends to encourage sensitivity to others, if not appreciation of differences.

By law, as you know, our public schools must mirror the racial composition of the communities in which they are located. We prioritize compliance that will allow us to offer the educational opportunities our students deserve.

Reassignment brings change, of course, and change is not always easy. The bus rides to and from school may be longer, for example. Some students and parents may prefer the local school. As a result, we will gather as a committee to receive *hardship preferences* governing students' continuing in their local neighborhood school. The form for submission and future meeting(s) will be the subject of another correspondence.

For now, please wait until we know your child's school placement so that we can talk about specifics. Presenting both the positives and negatives to the children will help them to handle the effects of the reassignment. Students know but should be reminded that adults close to them at home and in school are available to facilitate the new challenges ahead.

The board members and I can assure you that we will continue to maintain our emphasis on an exceptionally high-quality educational experience for all of our district students. Our teachers look forward to maintaining District 20's good student-teacher ratio. Let us also be proud of the supplemental services we offer and the extra resources, tutorials, the before-school and after-school programs, and our continued commitment districtwide to students' reaching the state and national norms in testing. Reassignment still allows us to dovetail educational experiences with students' needs. Our students' learning is our most important objective.

We are aware of the university research indicating that both student achievement and social behavior of nonwhite school populations change for the better in classrooms with diverse student populations.

Please feel free to call me with your questions and concerns. I look forward to this new school year, even though it is several months away. I anticipate and am grateful for your support of our School District 20 and your children's success.

Sincerely,

Chapter Thirteen

Some Parents' Concerns Lead to the Desire to Enroll Their Children in Private and Parochial Schools

The crisis: As a result of the reassignment plan, a group of District 20 parents met to explore other school alternatives. They started with an examination of the private and/or parochial schools available. The district superintendent, similarly concerned, was led to review the opportunities offered. This letter came out of her concern that parents receive additional information.

Dear Parents/Guardians,

Please allow me to respond to the Committee of Five and other parents seeking educational opportunities beyond our district in the wake of the reassignment plan. Our stipulated goal is to balance our schools' enrollments and create close to ideally sized classes that allow teachers to individualize instruction in our four elementary schools.

The committee members and others have told me about their inquiries and initial assessment of private and parochial school alternatives, and I want to provide another view of these. We have interviewed a number of teachers from both private and parochial schools for district positions; one question usually asked is why they want to leave their current schools. Some concerns surface in interviews, as covered below.

As you might know, youths must start team and individual sports as early as their interests begin. Sports are highly competitive at the middle and high school levels. Check what sports are available at high-tuition private and parochial schools. Are their coaches qualified? What are their facilities like? Can they match our sports readiness programs?

We maintain a district commitment to improve learning opportunities for students that include tutors, computers in every classroom, supplemental book sources, and changing resource center programs as needed. Note what services and supplementals are routine in the schools you are interested in. Which out-of-class offerings emphasize units taught in the major subjects?

Where do your tax dollars go? Our district business manager publishes reports breaking down the district's yearly budget. What will your tuition pay for in the private or parochial school?

Check the class sizes for all subjects: plan to visit when the schools are in session. Ask what the pupil/teacher ratio is.

Teachers tend to utilize a variety of worksheets, exercises, outlines, schedules, lecture notes, and so forth. In some parochial schools, instructors are limited in terms of the number of duplicated materials *allowed*. Check with a few teachers at these schools. Do administrators monitor the number and use of handouts to supplement daily lessons?

What do the library and resource center look like? Are there facilities for tutoring and supplemental work with students? How many volumes are available in the library? What is your impression of the computer center? The media center?

How many school counselors are available? What is the ratio of students to counselors?

Are all instructors certified in this state or in the process of becoming state-certified instructors?

Where after-school activities and team practices are available, what transportation exists for students to get home after activities? In one private school, parents were responsible for driving their children home after practices.

Determine the school's accreditation status and request a report thereof. You may find only private colleges and university departments with a similar philosophy and/or beliefs evaluate these schools. Is that appropriate? Their rankings may be based on comparisons only with other private and parochial schools, for example.

What are the accelerated programs like? Are courses available for gifted and talented students in math, English, science, and social sciences?

Note the number of students in the cafeterias and recreational areas. Do students have access to grade-level lounges or open gyms, for example?

Visit the offices of the teachers of the four major subjects. You may discover few teachers have their own offices.

I know you will thoroughly evaluate all educational opportunities for your children. My concern is that you compare and contrast our programs and services to parochial and private schools so that you will make a knowledgeable decision. Our schools are state-recognized for a consistently high level of academic study and *superior* preparation for students entering middle and high schools. Can the parochial or private schools compare and compete with us?

Please let me know if I can answer any questions you have about what we offer our students.

Sincerely,

Chapter Fourteen

"The Administrator's Focus" (Title of Monthly Feature)

(Local Newspaper Column Informs Stakeholders)

Let me review some of the events scheduled to occur during this school term.

- Recycle bins to be moved
  Some of the waste disposal employees have graciously offered to move the three recycling containers from the front of our school. The relocation site is the original Home Avenue location, behind the Methodist church. Our building evaluators with the Appearance Subcommittee agreed the receptacles were an eyesore, detracting from a "positive overall first impression" of our school and campus.
- Clean-Up Campaign
  School personnel will spend one Saturday, weather permitting, assisting the Hawkshead Spruce Up, Clean Up event. Volunteers can choose to help around the river area, downtown, on factory row, targeted neighborhoods, or Highway 90. Since our board members will join us in this community effort, please plan to attend: This is a big undertaking.
  Please sign up by calling in at town hall; the committee members want to provide snacks and beverages for all who pitch in.
- Testing
  With our overall improvement in end-of-grade testing as an inescapable goal in our district, we will host a Taskforce on Testing Panel. Member/experts will answer questions and provide suggestions.
  We will meet as a district group in Lincoln Junior High School's cafeteria, with required attendance of all faculty members. This will be our upcoming half-day institute focus.
- Sensitivity Session
  The district daylong institute topic is Sensitizing School Personnel to New Minority Populations. National experts will offer perspectives under the

category titles Values, Culture, and Identity. Since our district schools continue to enroll high numbers of minority populations, we need to update our awareness of techniques that facilitate achievement and a positive academic experience for newcomers of all socioeconomic levels.

Group leaders/experts will share research about varying cultures among specific populations and effective school practices to meet these students' needs.

- State University Assessment

Although we have been evaluated by other sources, we have not experienced a university team of experts looking at school climate in terms of the influence on student achievement. This component may satisfy an overall objective related to assessment by external evaluators.

I am, of course, interested in any informal suggestions you may have; please take the time to write your impressions, suggestions, and perspectives on the topic. Research indicates school climate is a key factor in students' academic success, as you may know.

Chapter Fifteen

Students Who Verbalize Their Beliefs or Evangelize

The crisis: Parents have called the district office expressing concerns about students who bring their strong religious convictions to school, attempting to ascertain other students' beliefs with the intent to save them. Others sometimes adamantly explain their beliefs and ideas during class sessions.

Dear Parents/Guardians,

Perhaps one of the greatest strengths in our school district is its diversity. We are proud to prepare our young people for their world experiences. Because we are also semi-urban, all of us are more aware of the wide range of ethnic and religious beliefs as well as some of the customs and holidays observed by various members of our school community [states the value of school community diversity, leading up to the requested respect for everyone, each in his/her own beliefs].

American public education is nonsectarian, as you know. We cannot forget that our respect for others includes advocating our own beliefs only during free time, lunch hours, and before and after school. Proclaiming, publicizing, or asserting individual points of view, even when representing local houses of faith, is not encouraged. Handing out materials is acceptable only when the receiver is receptive. Those who listen are not obligated to accept pamphlets and the like [definition of the problem: advocating one set of beliefs over others; also discouraging the distribution of tracts or pamphlets if students to whom they are directed do not want them].

Recently, some of our middle-school students urged classmates to attend their chosen congregation during a class. Somehow the students believed there was a connection to what they were reading as a class assignment, despite the fact that the instructor did not encourage the tie-in. Warning others whom an individual student perceives "need help" is not usually received well, regardless of the worthy intentions of the speaker. Similarly, promising *to save* a classmate even when a classmate has not approached or asked about one's beliefs and/or congregation must be regarded as out of place in our buildings. Offering free Bibles is also out of place, but carrying one and reading it in free time is strictly up to the individual student [identifies problem with specifics].

Students are advised to approach their parents about the appropriateness of advocating and prioritizing their own strong beliefs or their membership in a specific congregation before engaging other students. Advise your children about their rights and other students' rights and responsibilities in and outside of classes and on bus rides to and from home [suggests parents' intervention, explanation].

The order of our buildings, our attention to the educational tasks at hand, and our observance of a basic respect for others and their beliefs are important.

We ask for your assistance in explaining and emphasizing to your children that bringing personal religious beliefs into the school setting may violate other students' rights and is therefore not always acceptable. Urge, if you would, their sensitivity to the multicultural heritage that characterizes this area as well as America's history and society. Our democracy is based on the right of all citizens to believe and worship or not as they wish [allows parents to handle the topic with their own youngsters, plus offers an explanation of freedom for all to believe and practice as they are accustomed to].

Guidance staff in each building are aware that strong religious beliefs characterize many individuals in this geographic area. They recommend and I concur that the tendency of our young people to embrace and share new ideas not be squelched but avoided in the context of classroom instruction and activities. We value your input to guidance personnel and/or any of our administrative staff [open the issue to guidance counselors' help and their reception of feedback, as is true of school leaders].

Thank you for understanding our school situation. You are the best source of explanations related to faith, and I know you will handle your children's questions and concerns as they arise. Again, any staff member or I would be happy to talk with you or to assist you in this matter.

Sincerely,

Chapter Sixteen

Instructor's Leave of Absence

The crisis: Coach and Music Department staff member Scott Tyndall resigns. One of the school's most popular teachers, Tyndall excelled in all aspects of music and music instruction. A gifted instrumentalist, he brought musicals back into the school and also generated rare enthusiasm among students for band activities, stage production, and set design and choral activities. A new instructor will be hired to assume Mr. Tyndall's schedule and extracurricular responsibilities as soon as possible. (Rumors have circulated in the high school about an alleged romantic relationship between Mr. Tyndall and a student he coached in voice. An investigation is in progress.)

Dear Parents/Guardians and Students,

Our Delan School District 100 Board of Education and I received and accepted the resignation of Mr. Scott Tyndall of the Music Department late yesterday. Mr. Tyndall's desire to pursue other avenues of interest coincided with the availability of a professional opportunity out of state.

Superintendent Dr. Zweig has contacted a number of available candidates to fill Mr. Tyndall's position. Let me assure you we have four outstanding individuals whom we will interview this weekend. We, of course, seek an instructor who will provide both a seamless transition for students and a strong commitment to continuing our extracurricular music program.

In the interim, we remind you and all music students that our temporary substitute instructors are extremely well qualified, since we draw from Forest College graduate student music majors. Forest's reputation for music instruction is, of course, known throughout this country and in Europe.

I anticipate the faculty appointment will be filled shortly, but please let me know if I can be of any assistance in the meantime. We will maintain the schedule of practices, rehearsals, and lessons, as previously planned, with our capable substitutes in charge. These individuals may continue coaching and directing part-time, as needed.

Sincerely,

Tone: serious, authoritative, businesslike
Content: factual, explanatory, avoids the mention of rumors in view of legal issues
Organization: most important ideas precede those of lesser importance
Opener: immediate response to quell rumors
Audience: faculty, staff, local press, parents, and students

Chapter Seventeen

Student Deaths

The crisis: Three students died in a car accident.

Dear Parents/Guardians and Students,

Because every member of our Hillsboro School community is both valued and important, the loss of one individual who cannot be replaced alters the community. We are devastated by the deaths of three members of our school.

A loss of life due to other than natural causes always comes as a shock and a reminder of how fragile life is. Hillsboro is not the same.

Our hearts and remembrances go out to the families of Gerald Evans, Mitch Mackie, and Devon Williams.

School is not the usual place for mourning losses such as these—untimely and unexpected—yet we want to remember our own. Opportunities to do so will be described in succeeding paragraphs of this letter.

We are preparing a memory book for the family members of Gerald, Mitch, and Devon. Please consider composing something you especially remember about any or all of these three fine young men. We will collect your messages and arrange for professional binding. Please leave all memory pieces in Guidance with Mrs. Tuttle. Give us the leeway of several days to collect and bind the selections. Next Friday, we plan to present the collection of notes and memories, cards, and artwork to the individual families.

Please join us in our school gathering honoring these deceased athletes at the assembly in the gymnasium Wednesday morning at 9 A.M. Counselors, teachers, administrators, and support personnel will speak about the students and then turn the assembly over to you students, led by junior Jeff David.

We invite you to speak if you choose to do so. Plan to join the line, which will form in back of the stage, with access in the hall adjacent to Room A102.

The Reverend Dwight Johnston will lead our formal memorial service, also in the gymnasium, after our memorials and a brief recess. Our service should last about an hour, and school buses will depart about 1 p.m.

School will not be in session tomorrow, Thursday, October 15. On Friday, our regularly scheduled classes and activities will resume. We will reschedule all Thursday events, as needed.

Friends are also welcome to attend a church memorial service Thursday at Bethany Benevolent on Town Square at 4:30 p.m.

It is difficult for all of us to bid these young men good-bye; we will help one another accordingly.

Mr. and Mrs. Evans and family, Ms. Mackie and her close relatives, and Mr. and Mrs. Williams will appreciate your recollections about their children.

Please feel free to approach any of us with questions or comments and concerns.

My door is always open to you, more so at this sad time. So let us help one another.

Sincerely,

Chapter Eighteen

Changes in the Alternative Placement School-within-the-School

The crisis: The Alternative School for suspended students acquired a negative reputation, and yet administrators, faculty, and Guidance Department members felt it seemed like too good an idea to drop. Would changes help, they wondered? One strong element was offering students key components of change: keeping them from repeating suspensions; seeing their attitudes, self-image, and expectations change as a result of one-on-one meetings; and reviewing study skills and any other academic or classroom problems through meetings/discussions with counselors and staff supervisors.

Dear Parents/Guardians and Students,

A suspension is a serious matter, and our goal for Vernon High School students is to relocate those who have been suspended to a section of the building away from distractions, to review each student's individual goals, assess current study skills, and discuss the value of academic success in terms of current and future academic pursuits or training in a field of interest [purpose of letter is to explain new school-within-a-school but also mention program components].

Alternative Placement School assumes a new name, the Community School, and new location in the west wing of the building. Suspended students will have opportunities to recommit and to join their current classes via one-on-one discussions with selected adults during the suspensions [adult and student discussions tailor the experience toward a positive outcome].

Students will again complete their daily assignments under supervision.

We will stress the importance of success strategies, including attending class regularly, participating daily, utilizing a study schedule, maintaining an attitude of renewed achievement, and taking pride in finished assignments. Ongoing help with academic enrichment and/or remediation and discussions will occur with coaches, academic instructors, and counselors [steps to encourage student success].

We will include in-depth assessments and discussions with current academic teachers, plus supplemental materials as needed or suggested. We plan to provide tutors, if necessary. We will review test-taking. As a result, students will all have varied responsibilities for the duration of the suspension. But as a result they will know their strengths as well as weaknesses and will have a new focus on continuing to practice what they have learned when they return to their classes [provisions for students' success].

Parent feedback will be ongoing and is a requirement for students' entry into the Community School as well as the exit interviews and resumption of each student's regular classes once again [new focus on engaging parents in students' academics].

The components mentioned—counselors, tutors, supplemental materials, study skills assessment and review, test-taking strategies, appropriate attitude, and a *success mentality*, plus parent involvement—have shown in research data related to these programs and related ones that "higher than expected renewal and achievement" result. The majority of students interviewed and *followed up* for the semester after this type of program verbalized the cessation of nonproductive activities and replacement with new, positive responses to personal goals and academic achievement [research indicates success in school settings].

In addition to the school deans, parents, and teachers, our coaches or guidance personnel may initiate inquiry into the program's suitability for a specific student, even those who are not necessarily suspended. Some students simply need to shift their focus in school [school personnel may intervene for students who seem to need additional help provided by the Community School].

The Community School Program Director, Mrs. Alberta O. Davis, is available to talk with students and parents, faculty and staff, and guidance personnel. I am committed to Vernon students' success and I am enthused about our new lifeline to suspended students. We are utilizing our local university's College of Education to help assess the program and its results over the next four years [important components: director who oversees, plus results-oriented research].

This letter has been lengthy, but I hope it explains some of our new efforts directed toward student achievement and success. That is our goal at Vernon in order to prepare youths for what is ahead: future training or continued study, or work experience in their fields of interest. All of us involved in the Community School are enthusiastic about the concept and its potential to help students achieve at their best level.

Sincerely,

Chapter Nineteen

Superintendent's Internal Bulletin (Bulletin Requesting Information for Stakeholders)

Compiling a Comprehensive Public Relations Document on District Schools

To: District Faculty and Staff members

From: J. C. Jessup

Subject: A public-relations document: We are behind schedule on this one!

A realtor came to our office recently and told me she and her husband had just transferred to our community. They live in Manchester, in the Falls area, and she asked for a copy of our public relations material to share with her clients. She is a new team member of Hudson Valley Realtors.

Although we may hire a public relations specialist for the final draft, it is desirable for us to highlight the best features of our school district. Home values, as you know, are influenced by the prestige of a community; we need to inform our communities about our educational efforts. As a group, we are very likely to evolve a comprehensive overview of the district.

In the next four weeks, I ask that you compile a list of features you would include in a sample public relations document. Think of a brochure or pamphlet, a large slick-paper compilation with a cardboard cover, or whatever form you believe the information should take.

This is an opportunity to highlight what we do well. I am listing some topics to start your thinking process. I will, of course, look forward to these in any form you wish to send me. If you want to work in groups instead, feel free to do so.

The numbers: our numbers of graduates enrolled in education beyond high school
Reading programs, writing sequences
Science and mathematics distinctions, awards, and recognitions

Your department's most outstanding achievements

National test scores

Other awards, honors and distinctions, scholarships, foundation grants

Curriculums that are "documents of the future"

Extra help provided: tutors, catch-up courses, programs and services above and beyond classroom instruction

Details about the core curriculum and its results

Staff member recognition, state and national

Sports achievements (all sports)

Evidence of our district philosophy in action

Physical facilities (the pool, refurbished basketball gym, stadium improvements, hall of photos, historical milestones, etc.)

Chapter Twenty

Students Who Take Drugs

The crisis: The availability of drugs and the number of dealers who want to get youths addicted to whatever substances they sell are staggering, reaching into every single community in this country. And yet parents and teachers often reveal they had no knowledge that specific individuals were taking drugs. Instead, they attributed changes they saw in their children to moods or struggles to growing up, or to conflicts at school or in extracurricular activities.

Dear Parents/Guardians,

As you may have read in our community newspaper, police recently broke up and shut down methamphetamine labs in both the Ridge Hollow and Overlook communities. Although a total of six arrests means six fewer dealers in our area, none of us can become complacent about the availability of drugs. Police Captain Duval insists two other labs will almost surely replace these somewhere, in our community or one nearby.

Drugs are addictive and often impair one's judgment, if not alter the personality, yet inexperienced youths reveal that they feel empowered and confident when drugs are in their systems. Some young people are easily drawn to substances they think will permanently help them feel better about themselves and their problems as they experience new responsibilities in school, in extracurricular activities, in sports, and at home.

Pay special attention to your son and/or daughter's behavior and attitudes. There are signs that warrant your attention. A sudden lack of interest in classes and in other academic responsibilities may occur, or withdrawing from previously enjoyable extracurricular activities. If a negative progress report or a call from a teacher reveals a student's declining interest in a subject or in completing required assignments, follow up and call all teachers and activity sponsors or coaches who are familiar with your child. Begin a dialogue to monitor and/or identify specific problems and solutions. More often than not, your inquiries will be handled discreetly and will take little time, but they may offer important feedback. Of course, talk with your child in as objective a manner as you can, but express your concern and desire to help.

Is there a new group of friends with whom your child is spending time? Do you know them? Have they visited your home? Do you have any concerns about them? Have you met their parents? Have you not seen your son or daughter's friends from last year or this past summer?

Edginess, overreactions, protests and denials, high-to-low moods, defiance or accusations of your hounding or harassing or not trusting the young person are signs that something is not right. These reactions can indicate experimentation with controlled substances, if not other concerns. Also, youths who suddenly spend long stretches of time alone and at a distance from family members could be potential signs of trouble. On the other hand, students between sixth and ninth grade experience many confusing changes associated with growing up.

Our school psychologist, Dr. Corinne Lawrence, specializes in analyzing and clarifying teens' problems with them. Students enjoy her up-front honesty and her listening to them, respecting their point of view. Hers is a "no-nonsense" approach based on clear delineation of problems and the exploration of help and solutions.

We can, of course, recommend other qualified professionals within this community and surrounding locations, professionals who intervene when youths experience emotional distress or show lack of interest or other sudden changes in behavior or declining interest in academics and previous goals.

Our district personnel take pride in educating students, but above all we care about them as individuals and want to facilitate their personal growth as well as academic progress. Feel free to call me about any concerns you have related to this letter. I keep an open time between 1 and 2 p.m. daily, strictly for parents' calls.

Just to repeat an important point: granted, behavior changes may occur with growing up and meeting new challenges and are not to be confused with a youth's sudden interest in drugs. But let's verify that for ourselves and utilize Dr. Lawrence's help, as indicated.

Sincerely,

Chapter Twenty-One

(Sometimes Problematic) Parents

The crisis: Sometimes it seems parents are tougher to deal with than ever before. Teachers report their sometimes critical, hostile attitudes; expectations of altering assignment or test deadlines to meet personal or family schedules; and frequent e-mails and phone calls. Parents have been known to demand, cry, threaten, and/or accuse in a high-handed manner. "We pay your salary" somehow seems to justify their behavior, as though teachers are servants. On the other hand, the stakes are high: their expectations of children as well as teachers may be unrealistic.

Dear Parents/Guardians,

We are fortunate that the semester is going well so far in all of our buildings. Administrators and faculty have high hopes for improved results on the end-of-grade tests: our teachers spent a good deal of time this summer reviewing course objectives, researching and discussing new teaching and learning options guided by the objectives, and finalizing new course project ideas and new independent study options for many classes.

I have a few reminders and concerns to share with you, however. Although this letter is lengthy, I ask you to read it carefully. Thanks for your cooperation and help.

Coursework and Tests

Teachers set their own policies on the assignments and tests keyed to the course goals. They determine makeup policies. If students are absent on a test day (and we are now flagging these numbers on absentee lists so we have figures to work with), their makeup exam may not be the same test as the other students'. That is the individual instructor's prerogative, of course.

Most of our instructors pass out weekly or monthly schedules or plans, listing daily work due and highlighting test days. Your child learns to assume a high level of responsibility for learning—completing assignments on time, participating in class as indicated, working in groups, and reviewing in preparation for tests. We want it that way.

Research shows these are good habits to acquire now and for future responsibilities.

E-mail, Phone Calls

Our teachers usually have after-school work, whether coaching or assisting, meeting with department chairs, planning units with other teachers, monitoring students in club meetings or intramural events, serving on committees, evaluating course content, attending professional enrichments as offered—you get the idea. The list is long.

When our teachers get home, their workday does not stop. They must review students' homework, grade papers, tests, or quizzes, plan for the next day, assemble additional materials for the rest of the week, and review each textbook assignment or worksheet, as assigned. Most teachers have families and additional personal responsibilities.

I ask you to keep e-mails and phone calls to teachers at a minimum, if possible. They are carrying heavy loads as it is. That preparation for the next day comes first, unless your message is an emergency. Give them time to get their lesson plans done for the next day, and please remember that many teachers have two or three preparations.

Student Absences

Our students miss a full lesson each time they are absent. Try to monitor absences as carefully as you can; it is best that students be in class, every class. That is their responsibility and they will do better academically if they follow the schedule in each class day-by-day and prioritize daily attendance.

Individual Criticisms

Teachers rarely *pick on* a student. Neither you nor I was in the room at the time a problem surfaced, so let's hear both sides of an issue if your child and the teacher cannot solve a problem. I want as little involvement in a teacher's use of class time as possible, and I do not approve of hovering in the hallways to monitor their class periods.

Our teachers are gifted, experienced educators; let's support them in any way we can. Your children will pick up on your appreciation and support of teachers' individual efforts and policies. That's a good thing.

Respect

They perform a public service, and teachers are due the utmost respect from all of us. Just a reminder here: Sarcasm or criticism is out of line when speaking with our faculty and staff as well as any other employee of the district, but questions or comments delivered in a normal speaking tone are always preferred. We teach youths how to treat others by our example. I hope we want to set good examples when we contact any of our professionals on staff.

Similarly, please avoid telling or ordering individual teachers to do one thing and another. Recall, they set the assignments, readings, and test days. If a class exercise covered an entire outline, we do not expect our instructors to replicate the entire class period for a student who is absent. You must help at times to have your child here each and every day; there is little leeway on this. Learning is a daily effort in schools.

Teachers respect students and parents when students and parents respect them. I can assure you that our teachers will go that extra mile to see your child succeed. That's one of the primary reasons they choose the teaching profession.

Supplemental Services

We offer tutorials in all subjects and a resource center open all lunch periods and before and after school so that students can consult and ask questions one-on-one in a private office setting. This is true for all departments. Individual teachers are also available for appointments, at students' convenience and also at yours.

Our counselors belong to state and national organizations and are awarded recognition year after year for their outstanding service. They are also available for consultation with you and/or with your child whenever necessary. Give them a call if you are concerned about your child's progress.

Students' Responsibilities

I like to think that the following requirements are of concern to both you and your child:

- Attentiveness, engagement in class; asking questions or answering at least one question per period. Students must let each teacher know they want to learn!
- Taking notes in a notebook or on an outline each day of class: How else can they keep up?
- Completing all homework assignments, when due, with no omissions and no late assignments; log assignments in a notebook
- Avoidance of talking out loud, disrupting a lesson, or engaging other students in nonproductive conversations

- Completing the daily goal or activity in every class, and
- Realizing each student's behavior will be reported on a daily basis. Many teachers keep a dated behavioral log in their grade books. Behavior does influence learning: Is your child attentive and on-task? How do you know?

Spending time with your son or daughter to talk over their day in school, obtaining their feedback about each and every class, is something we cannot provide here at school. You also need to set aside and equip, as needed, the best possible study area for each of your children and a specific time limit, depending on their ages. Monitor what they are doing; encourage their efforts. Your children face more academic challenges with each year of school, and end-of-grade testing awaits all our district students. But you can help them to be responsible and ready to progress in all subject areas.

Students' success starts here, with their accountability, in school. You strengthen their opportunities for success with your approach to homework, studying, completing projects and, in general, preparing for each class every single day.

Our superintendent and board members do not subscribe to the philosophy that every class requirement in every department must be questioned— thankfully, departmental committee groups have already taken care of that with thorough, rigorous assessment activities. We do not approve of challenging or trying to change assignments, deadline dates, test schedules, the due dates of projects, outlines, book reviews, and the like. We rely on our educators' expertise because in almost all cases we have seen their philosophies result in students learning and progressing, achieving at their own rates. Meeting their responsibilities as they occur and maintaining deadlines are the best possible habits for students' academic success.

As a final note: our district schools are safe and well run; they are organized for our educational purposes, and our supplemental activities and services are sources of pride. Safe schools like ours follow set procedures to maintain an orderly, appropriate environment. There is respect for each member of this school community. We try to keep each student on-task and managed by adults throughout our school day. If you have any questions about this or any other issues mentioned above, let me know.

I know I can count on you to support our teachers' fine educational efforts. Thank you for your interest.

Sincerely,

Chapter Twenty-Two

Spotlighting School Successes

If administrators and staff focus attention primarily on responses to crisis situations, they may undersell or overlook the many great things going on in their schools. Consider appointing a committee within each of the buildings to compile in written form the successes of students, faculty, and staff members. Good publicity outweighs the infrequent crises, whether the latter are handled very well or not.

Choose e-mail to all homes, board/district newsletter briefs, the superintendent's periodic reports, or fact sheets or copy to the Schools Editor at the local newspapers to let everyone know throughout the year whatever is a source of pride—whatever is going *right* in your district.

Taking pride in faculty and students' efforts is laudable, but also allow the highlights and high points of each month to call attention to your school. You don't need a public-relations representative; urge every member of the school community to write short descriptions of events, awards, progress, achievements, recognitions, and honors that others may not be aware of. A few ideas:

Sports records and successful seasons (besides the school and local newspaper coverage)

Students who are involved in sports for two or more years as well as newcomers who are valued members of specific teams

Awards, honors, and recognitions at the local, division, and state levels in the arts, sciences, languages, musical programs, clubs, plays, newspaper and yearbook contributions, as well as in competitions with other schools

Variety shows and plays

Homecoming activities, from planning all the way to the weekend game and dance

Club service projects and fund-raising events

Camera club recognition

Art shows

Plant sales conducted by the horticulture classes

Speech and debate activities

New or revised courses—and the results in terms of student successes

Computer knowledge and competition(s)

Foreign language activities, in and outside of classes

New educational opportunities in the talking stages at board meetings; let parents know the board members and district personnel strive to offer the best education for all students. Review the terms of education as they emerge; review the advantages and disadvantages of year-round schools, modular classrooms, block scheduling, split shifts, etc.

Trends in education, whether teaching strategies or new approaches that help students learn

Counselors' column: What's new or of interest besides the focus on important pre-college responsibilities?

Inquiries about new courses to offer to meet specific students' needs

Options available for remediation or relearning in each subject area

New state and/or federal legislation affecting education at various levels, and the district's responses

National Assessments, end-of-grade testing, Yearly Adequate Progress tests, and the like (a sample of a few questions from each as well as its purpose might be beneficial)

Service projects, school/community service or ties to the community (special speakers)

Board member interviews: their concerns, goals, and expectations as well as their personal messages to students

A debate on testing: too much or too important to miss?

Question-box-style input: any member of the school community may ask a question, whether a named or anonymous request. Example of a student question: Can you draw the connection between school and work later on? I just don't see it. (My dad owns his own business and I'll probably be in the business.)

Band, concert band, the Music Department's growth and offerings

Students' physical fitness: Has anyone conducted a study or polled students for opinions, concerns, and questions?

Chapter Twenty-Three

Graduation

The crisis: Chaotic, uncontrolled graduation ceremonies leave some students and guests with a negative memory of a very important occasion for families.

Dear Students (and Parents/Guardians),

In thirty days, our seniors become Northeast High School alumni; graduation is a significant milestone in each student's life.

Northeast's administrators and staff members prepare very carefully for this occasion—readying the gymnasium, ordering floral arrangements, arranging for printed programs with all of our speakers' remarks, hiring extra security monitors, and setting up closed-circuit television for the cafeteria in preparation for extra guests.

Members of the Northeast High School District 112 Board of Education assemble early on stage in preparation for this crowning event of the school year. They are happy to celebrate the occasion with you.

Each year, we assess the number of tickets requested in terms of the numbers of seats. Your parents and grandparents, aunts and uncles, and siblings are always welcome if we have room. We do our best to offer everyone gym seating, of course.

But graduation brings to mind a question we (staff members, faculty, and administrators) want you to think about: To whom is the graduation ceremony most important? Is it the graduates' parents and other family members? Our students and their friends? Based on the numbers of cameras and recorders we will see that night, I would guess it is a ceremony of importance to all the above, including our faculty, staff, administrators, and board members.

Did you know we have volunteer faculty and staff members as well as administrators who want to attend and help set up the gym as well as distribute programs and escort guests to their seats or assist with lining up the graduates and monitoring the proceedings once they start?

The ceremony recognizes each and every graduating senior as he/she walks across that stage and accepts the diploma. This year, 228 seniors will receive recognition.

Let me ask another question of our graduating students: Will your family members, friends, and relatives be proud of you? Will your behavior match the formality of this occasion? We are counting on you to observe the solemnity of this special evening. A lot of people will have come a long way to see the ceremony; many individuals have waited for this one night of your life. It is your graduation, of course. But if you think about it, each member of your family and all of your friends share the night with you.

We want to host a ceremony of dignity that accords each graduate adequate recognition. If this year's graduation is not the special occasion it should be, our security staff and faculty members in designated areas of the gymnasium will respond to any and all interruptions. The board and I agree that we should remove any disruptive individual who does not allow the audience to enjoy the occasion, who prevents the individual names announced from being heard, or who feels the need to shout out. We will utilize the exam rooms and study halls on the second and/or third floor for those who interrupt the ceremony in any way.

We owe you and all of your relatives and friends that one courtesy—your recognition in public as you receive your diploma. We want this to be an occasion you can be proud of for the rest of your life—and, believe me, you will look back on graduation day again and again. Please remember our expectations. I look forward to seeing you on graduation night.

Sincerely,

Chapter Twenty-Four

Superintendent's Letter to Community Members and Teaching Staff

Explanatory Letter Reviews Teachers' Dissatisfactions, Criticisms of Administrative Practices

Dear Fellow Community Members and the Teaching Staff of Unified District 56,
    I have received a number of phone calls from our villagers, and they concern me. I usually don't write what might be termed *open letters*, but I need to address the letter you may have gotten this past week. Apparently, an anonymous teacher in the district chose not to talk to me but to forward some complaints to you. At least hear me out.

Paychecks
    The complaint was that paychecks are not available until after school closes for the day on the thirtieth of the month. That's true. In the past, I've allowed distribution of paychecks only to discover any number of our instructors abandoning duty assignments in all three buildings (where we need them) to post their checks in the banks in town. If they were late coming back, that did not seem to bother them. The bank personnel said lunch hour was really popular with our employees, and around 3 p.m.
    We cannot have this. We need each and every teacher in the building the entire school day. That's what we pay for, a teacher's time, whether instructing or on various duty assignments.
    And it is true that the district pockets a day of interest on that money if it's carried on into the next day's posting. We're doing reasonably well financially. We could do better. This is no real hardship as I see it, if our faculty members plan ahead, knowing they won't count on the thirtieth as a post day.

Building Attendance Check-In
    Each building principal needs to know who is in the building. These are big buildings, with a lot of space to cover. The principals are usually handling

other matters: getting ready for the day, dealing with emergencies or parent calls, monitoring and walking the halls. They cannot be expected to check each attendance room and classroom.

The only way we know if school employees are in the building is their checking in on an attendance sheet, preferably in the main office. It does not seem a terrible inconvenience. I like to greet my staff personally if I am over in any of the offices. We have used this system for years and no one complained until now. It does not seem a hardship requirement to me . . . correct me if I am mistaken. I want to know who is present.

Faculty Meetings

Yes, Dean Glover checks off attendance at these required meetings. We have information to convey and will continue to monitor faculty attendance. Who could argue with this?

Duty Assignments, Extracurricular

Another hardship, apparently. Each member of the faculty receives a regular assignment to a home event, whether game, meet, drama presentation, variety show—any activity. We also require faculty members to assist security personnel as necessary. As you know, we have some rivalries with other schools that are potential problems we would just as soon avoid. The more adult faculty, the better, as I see it.

These are unpaid assignments. Giving up an evening or two per year saves this district money. A little belt-tightening is good for all of us; I usually attend each and every event I can, by the way. Serving as a ticket-taker, bleacher monitor, floor monitor, supervisor at the door, etc., is no real hardship for professionals. I've done it myself quite often. Or is it a hardship? You give me your opinion.

If you teachers cannot give one or two nights to the district that employs and pays you, I might suggest you check with other districts. They may have tough unions, but their systems are not perfect, either. You have no choice joining a union school, you know: they take their fee right out of your check before you get it.

Classroom Doors

This is a safety issue. If I'm in the halls, I check doors. I want to know which classroom doors are locked. It's serious: let's not give students a place to gather. I do follow up with a teacher who leaves a door unlocked. In these days, we cannot afford that kind of carelessness; someone may take advantage of it. Mr. Cahill and I have every right to check doors.

I can provide those big key chains so no one *forgets* to carry their key or the obligation to lock classroom doors. Our books, equipment, a teacher's personal belongings in the drawers, and the like cannot necessarily be replaced.

Personal Leave Day

We do give our employees two personal leave days. I have been accused of denying a personal leave to one individual who was OK'd by the building principal to take a specific day.

I got a call within the hour of receiving that request from Don McMasters in Norwood District. He wanted a recommendation on the employee who had applied for a teaching position in his district. It's a good district, nice area.

It is true that I turned this employee down after the principal OK'd it. The principal and I *both* have to OK those requests. Interviewing elsewhere and getting paid for the day here doesn't sit well with me. I may be old-fashioned, but I appreciate loyalty. How do you feel about that?

I do not mind being criticized for sloppy administrative practices, for creating busy work and a plethora of forms and surveys, for expecting professionalism and the highest standards of performance from employees. I do appreciate being called to task and openly complained about to the point of grievance if I cause genuine hardships in various requirements, especially as regards curriculum work, assessments and portfolios, fewer absence days, and expectations beyond the teaching day. The latter is sometimes necessary if we have an emergency, however.

I do not like to respond to this type of criticism and complaint because I work as hard as my district employees do, and if anyone gets to know me, they know I expect of others only what I expect of myself. As I see it, we need to be good examples to one another. There seems to be another side to every issue, so I hope I have put some of these concerns to rest with this overview.

If you need to talk with me, call me rather than drop by. I'm usually in the building rather than in my office. But I welcome your perceptions.

Sincerely,

Chapter Twenty-Five

Bus Behavior

The crisis: Students' unsafe and disruptive behavior on the school buses

Dear Parents/Guardians and Students,

Dean Gene Curtis advises me that five of our South Park Middle School students (all on different bus routes) will lose the privilege of riding the buses to and from school with only one more infraction, one more write-up. I want to utilize this opportunity to review some of the expectations of our riders, as follows:

1. The bus driver is the adult authority who takes the place of a parent or teacher. The driver expects respect from each rider.
2. A safe ride is a quiet ride so that the driver can hear messages from the base operator and listen for police or ambulance sirens. A driver should never be aware of individual conversations going on among bus riders.
3. An undisturbed ride with the driver in control will allow him/her to monitor traffic conditions, react to changes in traffic patterns or roadway hazards and accidents, and make the appropriate stops on the route.
4. The bus driver must take attendance twice on each run. Every student must respond to the attendance calls and also remain in the assigned seat the entire ride. No student should stand up until the bus stops and the door opens for exiting.
5. Student riders must avoid comments and behaviors that distract the bus driver, especially arguments, scuffles and horseplay, throwing things, appropriating another student's materials or belongings and passing them to other riders, etc.
6. There is no eating on the bus. Because of the assigned seating, we are aware of the individual students who have been smashing food on windows, in the aisle treads, around the seats and rear door, and in the back of the buses.

7. Bus drivers are always free to write up behavioral referrals on students who interfere with the safety and security of other students or the driver.

8. Referrals are taken seriously and follow-up always occurs, starting with a behavioral contract that must be adhered to pending loss of the bus privilege, in addition to calls home, and requests for parent conferences.

9. Bus drivers are permitted to defend themselves if their physical safety is in question or if a student or students compromise the operation of the bus.

10. Once a student is removed from a bus or the driver must stop the bus because of a rider's verbal abuse or physical disruption or display, the student loses the bus privilege for the remainder of the school year.

11. Throwing any object out of a bus window merits automatic loss of the bus privilege for the remainder of the school year as well as parent conferences and follow-up suspension.

A student threw a gym shoe out of one of our buses and hit a jogger last year. When the case came before the court, the judge was outraged by the student's audacity, and ruled in favor of the jogger who never ran that route again. The parents paid a significant fine for the behavior of their son. This year our drivers report students' behavior is more aggressive toward one another, and there are more verbal disruptions, with warnings from drivers that these interfere with safe, efficient bus rides. All drivers indicate they are reminding student riders about their behavior entirely too often.

Our bus drivers are keeping anecdotal records, dated, identifying students' behaviors. We will do whatever it takes to assure safe, secure rides for our students, even if it means withdrawing that privilege from some current riders whose only means of transportation is the bus.

Safe Yellow bus company executives are adamant about their refusal to allow misbehaving students a second chance, let alone a third. Safe Yellow's reputation and safety record, insist the owners, cannot be compromised. This is one company that can choose the schools whose students they want to accommodate to and from school, by the way.

I have been very frank with you here, but the issues of safety and student behavior are very serious. I would be happy to speak with you, as you desire.

Sincerely,

Chapter Twenty-Six

Superintendent's Newspaper Column about Security Officer

School Leader Addresses Stakeholders about Security Officer Position

If you think about the safety issues and challenges of our three district school buildings, you realize the importance of a key staff position. Graham Griffin, our District School Safety Manager of twenty-five years, retires in just a few months. Mr. Griffin offers his recommendation to hire as his replacement expeditiously or suggests that we allow the safety officers to overlap in function for a while. We may do the latter.

We appreciate Mr. Griffin's dedication and his analytical approach to solving our problems. He has addressed every safety and security problem as it arose and then recommended changes to implement, as needed, before moving on to the next concern. He put in more time than any of us; the chair in his office looks brand new. He has always been visible in our buildings. As a result, we have an excellent safety record.

The board members and our administrators concur with Mr. Griffin and the Concept Safe Schools program we follow in their recommendation of a full-time security officer for our size district. The specifications cite an individual who is experienced and dressed in uniform and armed, someone who understands and will address the issues our changing, burgeoning school population brings to this learning community. He will recognize what we may overlook as a safety concern.

Mr. Griffin suggested we talk with Mr. Walter Hufnagel, and I want to let you know a little bit about him. Self-described as "always moving," he feels his job is mobile: strolling, checking the buildings thoroughly; assessing; looking for gaps and solutions and utilizing his past experience. He was a member of the Alamo Police Department but missed his ties here in our community. He wants to make a difference in young people's lives, to "set them straight," if they need it.

Walter Hufnagel's goal is to get to know the students in all three buildings as well as faculty and staff members. He is interested in their concerns and questions, their perceptions and safety consciousness. Hufnagel wants to train each building's professionals to notice matters of safety and security as well as know how to approach a budding problem or solve one in progress. He envisions his job as an on-call effort 24 hours a day, every day, but he expects the long hours guarantee covering the job adequately.

He knows students will not "narc" on one another. Yet Hufnagel draws young adults like a magnet. He is no-nonsense, down-to-earth, a plain speaker and honest, up-front about everything. His gift is allowing young people to confide in him, to follow his advice. Moreover, he maintains ties with our local police department, having trained with some of the current officers. He has a good reputation and good experience.

To give an indication of his skills and prepare for our interview, Walt is ready to assess and offer to correct the factors that compromise our safety, or he will suggest modifications of or additions to the current school safety plan. He wants, of course, to walk each building with Graham Griffin. He is familiar with generating periodic reports, some intended for teachers, others directed to staff members, and still others to students.

He will cover the three schools in depth.

This is a full-time position, and Walt is eager to start his assessment. I couldn't ask for more. Graham Griffin concurs.

Chapter Twenty-Seven

A Student with a Weapon at School

The crisis: A student with no discipline record brings a weapon to school.

Dear Parents/Guardians and Students,

We reviewed our revised Milton Unit District student handbook and reread portions to our students in grade-level assemblies at the beginning of this year.

One important excerpt is as follows: "Any student who brings a weapon of any type (gun, hunting knife, an *ornamental* weapon, sword, hatchet, axe, box cutter) or any item that might be used to cause harm to another person when used as a weapon (a modified screwdriver, for example) will be suspended from school for the remainder of the school year." The handbook further advises parents that they must arrange for tutors or alternative school placement if the suspended student wants to progress with his/her classes.

One of our students in the middle school brought a gun to school Monday and displayed it. The weapon was promptly confiscated and a report filed with the police. Suspension of the student remains in effect.

We must follow through with every instance of weapons brought to school.

Administrators had stressed that there was no place whatsoever for any weapons in any of our buildings. If an individual student had any misgivings or questions about a weapon or tool, we advised students to leave the item at home.

Please review with your child that regardless of the intention "to just show it to my friends" or to use a weapon for a speech or art assignment—which I agree is hard to believe, though somewhat possible—bringing a weapon to school is still prohibited and the student doing so will be suspended. Even a penknife on a key chain should not be brought to school; it's a bladed item that can cause injury to others.

We cannot allow any weapons on campus, in any building, in any classroom. Please call me to discuss specific examples or incidents.

As you know, the safety and security of our buildings cannot be compromised. Not realizing or not knowing the district policy or consequences is not an excuse, as some parents claim. "He did not realize the gun was operative" is as unacceptable as "This old thing has not been fired since the turn of the century." It is not the student's intention that is the problem; bringing a weapon, any weapon, into a district school building is forbidden in all cases. All weapons are potential threats to our students' safety and security.

If you read the newspaper, you will realize that in Jamaica Gardens a student's family heirloom, reportedly a pirate's firearm, did indeed discharge accidentally when dropped (it was extraordinarily heavy). The student in that district's school had no harm in mind, but the gun might have killed someone.

Please review once again the district policy on weapons brought to school and the consequences. Please explain the consequences clearly, obtaining your child's promise not to violate this important rule. Monitor any weapons you own and keep them in locked cases and other secured areas since students are curious and want to see these.

I am available, of course, to you and your child for further discussion, as necessary. Your help is what we seek above all.

Sincerely,

Chapter Twenty-Eight

Death of an
Elementary Student's Mother

The crisis: An elementary student's family is shocked and saddened by the sudden death.

To: Teachers of Spring Valley Elementary School

From: Maddie Hunt, Principal

Mrs. Cassie Rogers, mother of Caryna Rogers (second grade, Mrs. Shelby), died unexpectedly during a routine, non-life-threatening surgical procedure yesterday.

Grief advisors tell us children recover from this event, though they remember the circumstances surrounding the death for the rest of their lives. They do not realize what has actually happened, simply that their mother is no longer in their lives. Caryna knows that her mother is suddenly *away*, though not realizing she will not come back. Her father has called a maternal aunt to stay with them at home for as long as necessary to help Caryna with this tragedy. He will take a leave of absence from work for his daughter's sake. He, of course, is devastated.

I encourage you to talk with your classes about what has happened. The children might want to compose notes or draw cards to Caryna; we will take them to the Rogers' home when we have collected batches of twenty or so or by class, as they are completed.

Also, explain to Caryna's friends that they may see responses to this loss from the young girl. Some children who are affected by a death may repeat a single phrase about it over and over again, as though verifying it. This includes such impressions as "She was asleep in the box" or "They put my mother into the ground."

Other children may explain the events surrounding the death, as "Auntie cooked dinner last night." They may say matter-of-factly, "Mommy is away. Where is she?" Our counselors will be ready for Caryna's return to school, but they plan to visit her at home several times before her return. We appreciate their efforts.

Please let me know about any suggestions you have to make this difficult time easier for the Rogers family. Any help you could offer would be welcome.

Caryna is bright and talented; losing her mother is a heartbreaking tragedy for all of us. But we need to care for Caryna as best we can, being unusually sensitive to her needs. I know you and our students will become influential in Caryna's healing.

Sincerely,

Chapter Twenty-Nine

Death of an Elementary Student's Older Brother

The crisis: The unexpected death of a brother whom the sibling idolized

To: Teachers of Emerson School (K–5)

From: Ella Summers, Principal
Ted Clemmons, the older brother of Jason (grade 5, Mr. Boyd's team), died in a rockslide. His lower body was crushed in a sudden torrent of rocks in the Canyon Mountain Pass area on last Saturday's Scout hike.

Ted and Jason were very close; Jason had spoken about being "just like him."

I ask that each of us do everything we can to help Jason. Visiting hours at O'Brien Funeral Home will be Wednesday, 1–3 p.m. We will allow classes or individual students to attend with their parents, as desired.

Everyone in Canyon City seemed to know the Clemmons family. Ted and Jason were both popular, well-liked.

Ted Senior and Irene express concern about making things easier for Jason. Mrs. Clemmons asked if I could suggest something, and I feel notes and letters are a possible choice, or a memory piece about Ted. Mr. and Mrs. Clemmons as well as Jason would appreciate this gesture, I am sure, but also if presented in a box or special folder that would be a keepsake for later on in life. Of course, personal letters of condolence or remembrance are always appreciated, even if too painful for the family to read at this time.

Reverend Harrington from the Church of God will be here at school Thursday at 10 a.m. to talk with all of our students in a special assembly. We have invited grief counselors and specialists to the assembly; they might also offer insights about how to deal with the loss and how to best help and respond to

Jason, and they may divide the audience into groups, as necessary. These counselors and guidance personnel have written about death and the reactions of youths to death as well as healing strategies. They come with very high recommendations.

This is a shock for all of us and so we anticipate recovery over time. But we have help here for the children if we are especially sensitive to each child's reactions in the aftermath of the tragic death.

If you have additional ideas that may help our children deal with the shock and loss of Ted Clemmons, please let me or the guidance specialists hear from you. Once again, I appreciate your efforts, especially at this time.

Sincerely,

Chapter Thirty

A High School Student's Suicide

The crisis: A loss of life at any age is a shock; it is even more tragic when a student ends his or her own life.

Dear Parents/Guardians of District 120 students,
"If we had only known . . ."
As a result of the letter sent home to you just days ago, I have received responses from a number of parents with comments about Hal Stanton's recent suicide.

Unfortunately, we can never predict a specific youth's potential for self-harm or suicide. However, we can be concerned and vigilant about our young people's school progress, their ideas, feelings and concerns, and their interactions with others.

You may know that our school leaders, faculty, and staff members participate in workshops, state and national conferences, and the university's lecture series on current educational issues, with relevance to local school problems and practices. We utilize follow-up sessions and share ideas at our staff meetings. We do research and invite experts to lead in-service sessions when desirable.

Please allow me to briefly share with you some of the concerns that were raised in last year's session on student self-harm.

Parental Pressure to Succeed
Some parents demand their children attain nearly perfect grades in all academic courses. Pressures on students may increase with the onset of college-level entry tests and scholarship opportunities and requirements. Getting into a preferred college or university almost becomes the single focus, if not preoccupation and worry, of both student and parents.

We have known parents who purchased a second set of school textbooks so that their freshman has a home copy of all books. There is an academic coach who visits with this family several times a month to report on requirements of various post-graduation schools, their programs, offerings, and requirements for admission. An adult tutor reviews the student's daily homework and supplies drills and additional exercises as needed for mastery. This student never rides the bus to and from school, for the family has hired a private driver for the year.

This is an extreme example, of course, but not totally unlikely to spread from one family to others, if not the case now.

Some students cannot handle the pressure to succeed generated by well-meaning parents. We must be sensitive to students who seem uncomfortable with parents' demands and expectations.

In reality, each high school student becomes interested when reading about and visiting his/her choice of post-secondary opportunities based on the pursuit of the Guidance Department's suggested research tools. The tools help individual students to isolate their academic strengths, potential related careers, and the requirements of a particular program of study, including internships and tours of a campus online. Guidance personnel take time to guide and talk with our students before their search begins.

An Ill-at-Ease Feeling

Each school has a mood, style, and atmosphere because it draws on and draws from the surrounding community its character and history, its residents, and its students, of course. In addition to socioeconomic realities, schools acquire reputations ("a great place to teach and learn," for example) and hold unique traditions in high esteem. Among the important distinctions might be a school's drama program, the football team's state standing, the number of graduates who enroll in Ivy League schools, national ranking based on test scores, and the like.

Students who move into the district may or may not feel they fit in. In addition, students who have lived in the district all of their lives may suddenly realize they are not comfortable with the values and pressures they perceive have shaped them. Some students are never accepted into the popular clique of students and take what they regard as rejection extremely seriously. A "too-smart" student who is more mature than others in classes stands out as different and also may not be accepted and welcomed by other students.

Some students enroll in private prep schools and cannot adjust because of a school's regimentation and overpowering tradition. They attend classes but are unhappy, lacking engagements with the material, teachers, and/or students. They feel they do not fit in even though their parents or relatives may have attended the school.

Isolates

Some students literally march to a different drummer, for whatever reason. Their maturity level, talents, and interests may isolate them. It might well be a specific hobby or talent unshared with others that sets them apart.

One high school junior was a professional model who spent many weekends in New York. Her portfolio showed photos of a very sophisticated, beautiful woman. Students disliked her; they did not understand her career responsibilities or her very urban style; they were critical of her and her responses in class. She got along well with all of the teachers instead of fellow students.

Some students who are isolated adjust by downplaying their skills and talents and focusing on others; they continue to succeed but refrain from sharing part(s) of their lives. Others are crushed that they don't fit in with other students, and carry painful memories of being excluded their entire lives. School experiences stay with them, and they never want to repeat what they have lived through, whether it is being excluded from school groups, looking or dressing differently than others, following their interests in the arts, sciences, specialty mathematics, etc., without sharing their interests with others, or having only a precious few likeminded friends.

Some students may also take personal relationships very seriously, whether they share their deepest thoughts and dreams with a member of the opposite sex or within a strong, long-lasting relationship with a pal of the same sex. Even so, when two individuals reach high school, they may choose different routes and the former friendship becomes just a memory.

We all need a balanced perspective about ourselves, our abilities, our place in school, and later, in society. No one will probably ever judge us as harshly as we judge ourselves. We are often unrealistic in our expectations and rigid critics of ourselves.

Schools are difficult to grow up in; the pressure to succeed and learn, to achieve and to realize a balance between academics and outside interests is intense. Some students never realize many of their peers go through similar experiences, even if they are popular and members of the elite groups.

Somehow we need to convey that school careers are very important, but that one can also balance academic study with enjoyable extracurricular interests and can pursue clubs, hobbies, and one's own talents outside of classes. Friends also add so much to our lives and support our growth; no one should miss out on close friendships.

A school's faculty, staff, and guidance personnel are good sources for help with problems when students feel they cannot confide in parents or friends. I hope our faculty and staff convey this to all students and make them feel we are ready to help if asked. It is part of all educators' jobs. Our students' growth is wonderful to watch and encourage. Each student has something to contribute to school and to society; we must do what we can to facilitate the development of the interests, talents, skills, and abilities of all our students.

I have additional news: We will begin a district round-table open-discussion series for all parents and school personnel at all levels who are interested in pursuing their concerns about our students and how we can help them throughout their school careers. We will meet twice a month and set our goals. We intend to formulate plans for programs and dialogue with students that will address their concerns before they act on their own, as Hal Stanton did. Our goal will be to change what is negative for students and identify those individuals who may need a mentor or an adult interested in him/her. There will be a bulletin describing the informal discussion series as we move on to create new opportunities to help students. Please think about joining us, if you would, parents. We welcome all input from our students, of course, in whatever form they wish to share their ideas. You will receive information about this discussion group in the next few weeks.

I appreciate your feedback and suggestions about this new opportunity to help students and to talk with other adults about their perceptions and to share insights.

Sincerely,

[Note the use of detail and explanation in this letter: the crisis circumstance is serious and calls for careful review.

This letter indicates this school's proactive response to crisis events, especially in starting a discussion series open to parents and others interested in providing feedback and exchanging ideas on this and other topics perceived as important.

School services are mentioned, including the Guidance Department and teachers familiar with resources devoted to educational issues.

The specific descriptions of students who may experience difficulty is detailed so that readers know a little more about some students exhibiting characteristics that suggest potential problems for the individual.]

Chapter Thirty-One

Potential Student Dropouts

The crisis: Prevention of students from dropping out of school, Program Adapt

Dear Parents/Guardians and Students,

As we prepare the buildings for the fall, the board members, faculty, and staff want to inform you about the new Adapt program we talked about last year.

Identifying our district students who do not seem to be succeeding academically, or doing as well as their test scores and abilities indicate they can, we continued to use the word *adapt*.

Program Adapt is this district's response to meeting the problem of the student dropout rate. Although it is not an overwhelming problem at this time, our administrators, board, and staff want to address the issue of students leaving school and to have plans ready to accommodate students' needs.

We ask students to adapt to our school programs and requirements, but this program will allow us to address students' individual needs, with the district adapting to their difficulties and also planning with them for successful completion of high school, with training or experience in an interest area.

Students drop out of high school for a number of reasons: lack of connection to a school or academics in general; extracurricular interests; low expectations of academic success; lack of strong partnerships between school staff and parents; the routine and requirements of schools; problems completing assignments; inefficient study skills and not testing well; low self-esteem; and even an inability to connect school and the workplace after graduation.

Adapt brings students, parents, and building staff members together to set new goals and create individualized schedules and outside programs for all students interested. Most participants will spend some time in two settings three or four times a week, at school and a work-related site.

The *work site* may be our community college, a local business relevant to individual students' skills and interests, a technical institute, a fine arts studio or conservatory, or a business run by a family member or relative. Whether it is apprentice training or on-the-job work and/or learning on a specific online site where a college or skill course is offered, we will adapt to the students' abilities and interests.

Students interested in Adapt will contract to succeed in both settings. School leaders and staff offer statistics to show that students engage and do well in both settings due to four important features. Program features include identification of students who are potential candidates with a specific career interest and/or talent; a series of conferences with the student, parents, administrators, guidance personnel, and teachers; a plan for success alternating academics and hands-on work and study; and contracting a program of specific responsibilities and evaluations at school and at work.

Adapt addresses students' need to define their future job goals and their skills, by matching school courses to a particular job or work goal or interest, and by contracts for success in completing work at both school and a job site, and in regular, ongoing assessments.

Project Adapt may give a student the experience necessary for success while in school by connecting academic learning and skills to work outside of school.

We know the potential for success with this program and are more than happy to answer any questions you have. We will gladly set up individual conference times with program personnel and our staff members if you wish. Call Adapt Coordinator Bert Mills for more details or to discuss your child's interests and school progress. His phone number here at school is listed at the bottom of this letter, with the numbers of other student service personnel.

Our district board members, administrators, and staff members are committed to adapting an academic program to a student's individual job and career goals. We have in place the elements of success built into the Adapt Program. The effectiveness of Adapt is that it is keyed to each student's needs academically and in career/job fields. Students define their goals related to jobs that fit their skills; they learn how to plan to get experience, and they train for that future job. Again, we welcome your inquiry.

Sincerely,

Chapter Thirty-Two

A Student Brawl

The crisis: An out-of-control group of students

Dear Parents/Guardians and Students,

This afternoon's altercation in the gym involved twelve to fifteen students, at least five of whom are our varsity basketball players. However, twenty-five or more students, onlookers, encouraged the disruption. The fight and the encouragement to continue are unusual coming from our students [explains the incident and numbers involved; comments that it is unusual, not an everyday event].

We have not pinpointed the cause of the altercation.

Coach Sanderson collapsed after scuffling with one student while trying to stop the disturbance. He was taken to Rose Hospital's Emergency Services Department and released an hour later [quells rumor with facts].

Police arrived within minutes of our calling them, and members of our security team, teachers, and other school support personnel raced to the gym when the Code Emergency One sounded throughout the building [designated signal brings school staff to the relevant area].

The adults stopped individual students by force, police held three of the five labeled *instigators* down on the floor, and teachers and staff members threatened expulsions for the rest of the year if the fighting continued. This could have been an out-of-control situation without the timely assistance of school personnel [explanation of actions taken].

The board of education members and I agree this kind of incident cannot recur; fights merit our most severe consequences. All of the students in the inner circle which started the melee will be suspended from school, pending the dean of students' meeting with individual students and their parents. Coach

Sanderson will call up another group of players to substitute for our varsity basketball team members against Marion Central and against other scheduled competitors, as necessary. All players involved in the incident—and we have not viewed our gymnasium's running security film sequence as yet—may well lose participation in the remainder of the season's games [severe penalty, suspension; meeting with parents, students, and dean; team players will have substitutes].

The student handbook specifies severe penalties when disruptions of this nature occur. There is no excuse for fighting or aiding those who are fighting, let alone verbally encouraging a group of students in conflict within our building, outside on school property, or in the location of athletic events [reinforces student handbook specifying expectations].

We expect the police personnel will confer with the dean and administrators, address the instigators of the disruption, and speak to all students in the building from the main office. We are fortunate that these men and women will go to this extent in order to see that situations like this one do not recur [police involvement highlights seriousness of the incident but desired compliance with rules on the part of students].

This is a first in my eight years here at Lawton High School, and I can guarantee you that it will not be a repeated event [principal's tone is unmistakable].

If you want to review or discuss any aspect of the incident that occurred today, please call me and I will get back to you.

Sincerely,

Chapter Thirty-Three

A Building Evacuation

The crisis: A serious circumstance threatens one district's students.

Dear Parents/Guardians and Students,

Administrators may not necessarily divulge the source of an emergency, but we expect student compliance with exit procedures, if authorized. This morning's phoned-in report of unspecified explosives in one of the buildings caused our three schools to evacuate. Two prior practice drills had seemed to run smoothly, with quiet, timely building exits.

We expected similar behavior today.

However, I must ask all parents to speak with your son or daughter if he/she attends either Whitcomb Middle or Truman High schools. Appropriate behavior and students' commitment to follow specific requests of building administrators and supervising teachers is mandatory, especially in evacuations. Students know the penalties are severe for lack of cooperation. A sixteen-week behavioral contract after noncompliance during an unusual event or circumstance is difficult for any student. Additional penalties may be levied; these circumstances are extremely serious.

We cannot allow students to take any emergency incident lightly; but loud talking, laughing and joking, and failure to follow adults' instructions all occurred this morning, to my dismay. If the threat had been genuine—and we never know this—there is no telling what might have occurred given the lighthearted atmosphere. Students must consider each emergency as a potential threat to each of them, and respond to it with seriousness.

As a result, we planned time-consuming class assemblies almost immediately to once again stress the specific rules to follow, appropriate behaviors, and the need for strict, quick compliance with adults' requests of students.

This includes responding to multiple roll calls, as needed. We must account for each and every student at all times. It is not a joking matter.

Our adult faculty and staff are responsible for reporting any and all students' behavioral and/or attitudinal problems to the dean of students, Dr. Sanders, for parent conferences and additional penalties, as necessary.

Please discuss the content of this letter with your son or daughter. I am available for questions, suggestions, and comments. Let me review the expectations we had during the emergency this morning:

1. Quiet attentiveness
2. Answering as many roll checks as expected
3. Lining up in the order specified by adult monitor or teacher
4. Moving away from the buildings to a site specified
5. Complying with adults' requests to face a specific direction away from a school building or remaining in a specific designated location, as assigned
6. Allowing Crisis Team members and fire and police departments to arrive and inspect buildings prior to an "All Clear" for reentry (middle school students)
7. Remaining with the partner assigned to each student for the duration of the emergency, until return to the classroom or parent pickup
8. Avoiding the burden of carrying cell phones, food, hand-sized games, radios, etc.

If your son or daughter hears it from school personnel and from you parents, they will in all likelihood realize the importance of following specific instructions.

Thank you for your help. These measures allow us to further guarantee the safety and well-being of all of our students.

Sincerely,

Chapter Thirty-Four

A Locker Search

The crisis: A student's locker draws a response from one member of a visiting police K-9 team; word quickly travels throughout the building that police are checking lockers.

Dear Parents/Guardians and Students,

An unexpected locker search yielded an unauthorized foreign substance—a drug in quantity apparently for selling—this morning on the first floor of our building. It was a fortuitous break for us that a K-9 police-trained dog and its trainer/handler were on-site, and on the first floor in the area of the auto shop and technical applications section.

Allow me to remind you that *probable cause* allows police to search any suspicious area, in this case pinpointed by Skip, a trained German shepherd and professional companion of Detective Sergeant Joseph Harris of Valley Police Department.

Skip and Sergeant Harris arrived to speak to Mrs. Meyer's class in that wing of the building. Unexpectedly, Skip's sniffing and sudden agitation when he approached a specific bank of lockers revealed the dog had detected something. Harris speculated at the time the lockers might all reveal lunch bags or other food.

The dog stopped dead and sat abruptly at one locker, though the sergeant led him along the entire row of lockers, one by one. Dean of Students Harrison arrived with a locker key when summoned, opened the specific locker the dog refused to move from, and the dog put its nose on what looked like an ordinary lunch bag. The bag contained a large amount of a powder substance, unidentified at that point, in four smaller bags. They were confiscated and marked for evidence purposes.

The student whose locker yielded the bag was called to the hallway, and Skip fixed his nose at the young man's left jacket pocket, which also contained a rolled-up paper bag containing what appeared to be the same powder substance in a small plastic bag within the larger one.

This is our first incident with drugs confiscated on school property, an offense that merits our most severe penalty and, of course, police intervention.

Sergeant Harris and Skip proceeded to Mrs. Meyer's class, and their talk was reportedly well-received.

Once again, let us refer you to the penalty for bringing foreign substances, including drugs, to school, as outlined in the student handbook. Sergeant Harris is now committed to searching all of our senior building lockers along with Skip, which is well within his job responsibilities. The searches will, of course, remain unannounced.

I am available for your comments and questions, as you know.

Sincerely,

Chapter Thirty-Five

A Fact Sheet for Media Representatives

Origin: Any School-Related Crisis Situation or Potential Crisis

As you know, one or more media representatives have a schools' beat, whether for the local or community newspaper or a television station. Their job is to report on any and all unusual incidents in school settings as well as to interview administrators and staff members who might provide them with a story they suspect is brewing.

Some school leaders feel that the media is entitled to a bare-bones brief; others, a one-on-one interview to answer what media representatives ask, if the answer does not impinge on an individual/individuals' rights or if they do not feel that withholding information is their prerogative. Media personnel have access to police reports, of course, and most reporters will research and probe a number of online sources and utilize any personal contacts they maintain before questioning school administrators.

Media representatives seek an interesting story in progress or a review of a story with a history as well as a first chance to cover/uncover brand-new or potentially dramatic or unusual material.

School leaders often receive regular calls from the media; providing them with a fact sheet saves time, unless a leader prefers to schedule an interview, whether to set the record straight or provide only specific information they want publicized.

The bare-bones fact sheet approach is illustrated in the following example, related to a prior entry about **a district's evacuation of its buildings**.

Middlebury Unit District 223

Phone number_____ Contact administrator_____

Event: Building Evacuations: elementary, middle school, high school

Origin: Phoned-in threat of "incendiary device" in one of the school buildings

Procedure, Process: Follow *routine* evacuation as practiced several times previously

Outcome: Local fire department special services team, building security staffs, and police search building by building; efficient, directed, thorough procedures. All move extremely quickly, as reported from within.

Time: Forty-five to fifty minutes total, with fire department, building, and police groups progressing from one school to another (each team covers each building in turn as a specialty team concludes one site and proceeds to the next).

Conclusion: Buildings declared "Clear, Safe"; classes reassemble to proceed with the day.

This covers the basic facts, which could be utilized to write a short release about the incident. It is left to the school reporter to ask whatever additional detail seems relevant. Reporters are accustomed to not receiving answers to all of their questions, but they will probe and are persistent in covering the areas readers might have questions about. School stories are of high interest to a large number of readers.

Chapter Thirty-Six

Yearly Proms

Potential crisis: Students eagerly anticipate their proms, but parents worry about what their children are doing, who their companions are, the threat of available alcohol, and the consequences of inappropriate choices should they occur.

Dear Parents/Guardians and Students,

As you know, students recently attended two highly effective student presentations urging our upperclassmen not to consume alcohol. The film clips and review of students' experiences offered all of us a frightening look at an uncontrolled prom evening and the day after. The sponsor and producer is the group Alcohol-Free Teens.

We have two final presentations within the next twelve weeks, almost guaranteed to convince students to stay alive, sober, worry-free, and stress-free. Some of it will shock students, but they need to see and know the outcomes of other students' choices.

What will follow the presentations are guest appearances of students connected with Alcohol-Free Teens; they will remain in our cafeteria all of one day (to be determined as yet) to talk to students, answer questions, and to offer them goodies and prizes.

The group will arrive early that day to display athletic team hats and T-shirt sets; gift certificates to the mall stores; athletic equipment; passes to concerts downtown; a large box of "college prep" items that they say contains everything you forgot when you arrive on campus; free movie rentals for home viewing; high-interest paperback books; stationery and pens; pens and pencils with their group's logo—and this is just what I have seen of the loot.

All our students need to do is take a pledge and sign and date the oath, agreeing to not drink or take drugs, now and in the future. They are given their selection of awards and prizes as displayed by the group. It is each student's choice, of course. Presenters with Alcohol-Free Teens have turned their lives around and offer testimony during the last two school meetings and then again on the cafeteria day. This emphasizes their decisions to abstain from alcohol and drugs, making the presentations more compelling.

Since we are looking ahead to the proms, this year ours will be jointly held at the Montauk Country Club, whose managers and staff offered us the facilities all of Saturday night and Sunday until 3 p.m. of the prom week. We administrators could not refuse their offer. They offer us free use of the facilities, which will be closed to all other individuals and groups during that weekend. So we've got a considerable number of community people apparently behind our effort to keep an eye on our students and yet give them an evening they'll hopefully enjoy and remember. If they do not enjoy this more than some fancy club, then they missed some great opportunities. Let me inform you what our students are getting with the Montauk evening and half-day.

Students will have a choice of club activities, for all club staff members have offered their services for the time period. Plus, we have recruited twenty or so of the fifty adult supervisors we want to attend and lend their presence to the celebration. First, the prom-goers can dance to the music of two different bands, local groups with high appeal and good reputations. They can also elect to enjoy the usual club offerings when they wish: tennis; swimming in one of the two pools; an elegant dining room dinner (three choices on the menu; an anonymous donor has already picked up the tab); dessert in the Parlor ice cream shop; and walks along the lighted paths around the lake on the property or in the club gardens. There will be continuous movies running in a theater they are setting up, and the Pro Shop, Notions gift store, and Cindy's Boutique will be open throughout the event for student purchases. It sounds inviting to me. The managers insist they are accustomed to big crowds and that they have comfortable seating for everyone involved in the evening; given the space the club has, I wouldn't doubt it. They'll set up a putting range and miniature golf course because their pro golfing facilities are off-limits (the only restriction on students).

Again, we will have fifty adults supervising the entire time, in shifts. Students may also recognize some familiar faces walking around and talking to them: we have invited pro golfers, local entertainers, alumni, a group of roving musicians, and even a few surprise guests whom I hope will attend.

Our proms' committee group is still talking about additional options, and if you can offer any other suggestions about more activities for this beautiful site or any other alternatives to fill the hours and provide the students with a great evening, please let me know. We will leak out enticing information about what will be available as the weekend grows closer, but for now, keep the plans outlined above to yourself.

Thanks for your interest in keeping our students safe and alcohol-free, plus newly committed not to drink or take drugs. We cannot refer to those two abstentions enough. The proms will be worth all of our efforts.

Sincerely,

Chapter Thirty-Seven

Gangs

Potential crisis: Gang activity or signs of affiliation cause concern.

Dear Parents/Guardians and Students,

Our local Bayshore Police Department personnel report that one or more gangs has our area targeted for infiltration; our community is *open* territory in their view, as the police tell me.

In view of this, you will notice more police in patrol cars present in town and in our neighborhoods. I am glad of it. We at Bayshore United School District 108 intend to greet any and all gang activity or recruitment in our community as unwelcome. We are committed to notifying police when we have suspicions or see signs of their presence. Let's all be vigilant about this threat.

We need your cooperation and assistance in our safety efforts.

Teachers, school personnel, and board members urge us to remind our students to report any individual who tries to recruit them to join unnamed others "for your own good" or "to turn a nice profit"—exact words. Gangs need cooperation and new members to stay active, to commit crimes, and to take the blame when things go wrong.

If you notice unfamiliar lettering, signs, symbols, and markings in prominent places, let the police or our security personnel know as soon as possible. It is important to isolate gang attempts to encroach and also to know which groups we may be dealing with. Gangs advertise, as you may know.

Also, if you see the floodlights around our schools, don't feel you have to call me: this is part of our security efforts. We are protecting the buildings.

If you see a suspicious group downtown or in your neighborhood, individuals whom you do not recognize, call the police to report where and when you saw them. Try to recall specifics: the exact number of individuals, what they were wearing, their activity, etc. Every detail may help police personnel.

Our young adults who may be somewhat dissatisfied with themselves, their friends, or their lives, and especially those who do not yet have abundant self-assurance or who enjoy feeling singled out as a member of what appears to be a powerful group, are sometimes easy recruits for gangs. Those students who are not engaged in school, clubs, sports, and the like may be at risk of joining a criminal group. Gang members will promise any recruit almost anything desired to get the person to join them in crimes. Of course, it is an entry on a police record almost immediately.

Gang members need a constant supply of young, naive recruits to steal, kill, or vandalize, and to supplement the group's numbers to look like they've got considerable size. To repeat the idea from above: they want to appear to be able to take over a community as they choose.

Make sure your son or daughter understands how gangs recruit and use members. According to Detective Brian Riley, "Gangs are trouble. They offer kids nothing but a police record and worthless promises of power. Join and you are headed for prison or six feet under. I can guarantee it; I have seen it." If you have any suspicions that your son or daughter has contacted or been approached by a gang, you might call Det. Riley to review what he knows about their members and activities, the violence they encourage, and the codes they espouse. Ask for his help as you need it. This experienced law enforcement officer is available to any of our students or their families.

If I can be of any help, please let me know. We will try to schedule class meetings or open assemblies to allow police experts to talk to our district youths about this new problem in the community.

Sincerely,

Chapter Thirty-Eight

Are Our Schools Safe?

How Did the Concern about the Safety of Their Schools Begin?

Potential crisis: A group of parents, aware of unsafe school conditions that they have read and heard about from national news sources, seeks to evolve a list of items indicating a particular district or individual school's commitment to/priority for safe schools. They want to (informally) assess their children's schools in this one area of concern.

A gathering of fifteen parents began a dialogue/discussion during a meeting for all members of the community interested in school safety. During the meeting, parent Darrel Lamont offered an idea. "Think of a continuum if you will, a line of two extremes. Label the left side *Dangerous* and the right side *Safe*. Then think about the safety features that characterize your child's school. I think in most cases we will discover our schools are safe. But school leaders might be interested in our perceptions of other features that concern us. Let's each write our own list and then share what we prioritized. But list safety features first, since I think this will prompt ideas about issues of concern, and then rank in order each of your list items on both sides of the continuum when you have completed the lists. What do you think? I've brought paper and pencils if you are interested."

Herb Williamson said quickly, "Now you're talking. This line idea gives all of us something to work for. *Continuum* I don't know. But I think you've got a good idea."

Below are the initial results, before their ranking of each item:

- Doors secured once students assemble for daily classes, then checked from the outside several times a day
- Existing, fully operational School or School District Safety Plan whose provisions are known by all who utilize the building(s). The plan has also been practice-tested in a drill more than one time.

- Chief security officer is a full-time staff member who has a number of other team members to monitor and who recommend action in the event of safety issue(s) of concern to the building occupants.
- Building personnel aware of and responsive to a variety of situations requiring a *safety alert*, such as a stranger in the building, a student carrying a weapon (may be a rumor but it must be checked out), the smell of smoke coming from an unknown room or area.
- A community safety team, an auxiliary unit that can arrive quickly at the school and whose members are on-call most of the day and evening (many run their own businesses or set their own work schedules)
- Students, faculty, and staff assume responsibility to report any suspicion of unsafe conditions or circumstances related to school safety. (Example: Mrs. Neal from the main office returned to her car for her eyeglasses one morning, taking a shortcut through the student parking lot, and noted what seemed to be a gun in a student's car. She followed up on her concern with the school's Security Chief Simpson.)
- Adult building monitors for all areas of a building, each one equipped with access to cell phones for school security purposes; monitors cover the building in their specified areas during their non-class times
- Schoolwide alert/warning tones or codes known by all students and staff members; breakdown of tones/code—full alert (someone or something exists as a threat); moderate or low-level (potential threat may exist or escalate, such as rumored tension between two groups of students); low-level or nonexistent threat alert ("Nothing unusual going on in guidance corridor," as one monitor reports, though he felt "It's too quiet down here.")
  Why have a low-level or nonexistent threat alert? The building's security team felt building occupants would know the usual *watch efforts* were in place; this would be an "Everything is OK" signal.
- Alerts are activated by verbal or written reports to specific school authorities and/or security staff. An alert also might take the form of a written report suggesting a specific hallway might be a scene for clandestine student meetings because of its isolated location; no one had noticed or mentioned this previously.
- School personnel apprised of individuals to contact with questions or concerns or perceived violations of safe school conditions
- Knowledge of, familiarity with evacuation procedures; lockdowns; procedures to report classroom doors open or unlocked; unsafe practices during lunch mods or in recreation areas; an accessible courtyard, for example, that is unsupervised—access should be limited to students with specific reason to gather there (legitimate or approved group's meeting, for example)
- Adherence to state or regional safety codes for schools, plus familiarity with suggestions about reporting suspicions (all who utilize school daily know these)
- Each adult in the building has in his/her possession a district or school's safety binder containing sheets of explanations of safety procedures and

practices, relevant articles, statistical studies of safe schools, etc.; listing of whom to call with various concerns (areas of responsibilities are designated to specific individuals); how to handle a situation, when meeting a stranger, for example, on one's assigned hall duty; forms and examples of written reports to alert safety officer to a specific concern or to ask a specific question that may be of interest to other adult monitors. Binder is reviewed, updated periodically.

- Attention to areas generally lacking regularly assigned safety personnel: band and music practice areas; shop and industrial wing; entrance areas in hallways to stage and auditorium, plus stage and auditorium; cafeteria and food preparation areas; determination of which are already monitored/safe areas, if possible
- Remote control from main office to individual rooms; sound system to check for presence of individuals in unmonitored classrooms or other areas (long hallway which is the length of the building leading to outside doors and parking lot, for example); rotating times daily for specific safety personnel to check rooms
- Assigned areas for safety/security teams to monitor during use by school teams who are competing; i.e., all sections of bleachers, snack stand, locker rooms, passageway from field to locker room, etc.; pinpointing other areas of concern during competitions
- Key or combination locks on all student lockers
- Safety information survey (a security assessment tool) completed yearly in each attendance or homeroom by all students and staff, with space for questions, comments, concerns. Surveys also go to all homes for parental input. Focus: building/district safety efforts and safety conditions.
- Periodic or twice-yearly reports from chief security officer directed to adults and students who utilize the building (an announcement, class meeting, review by classroom teachers, (selective) reproduction in principal or superintendent's newsletter, etc.)
- Professional safety assessment (police, security personnel, or other experts unfamiliar with specific practices of district who conduct walk-through unannounced); reports on file of their insights, concerns, recommendations to administrators, and the follow-up, as carried out
- Assessment of students' perceptions of their safety in school building and during athletic practices, meets, and other events—i.e., stage productions, art shows, plant sales, open houses, library book sales, etc.—many of which are open to the public
- Special safety procedures during construction or repair work when a section or sections of the building are open for workers' access. In one school, a teen drug dealer walked right into the high school and was selling substances between class periods, when all students were in the hallways moving to another class. A teacher tried to apprehend the seller, grabbing his jacket sleeve. The dealer simply walked out of the oversized leather jacket, leaving it in the teacher's hand.

- Maximum school safety practices and goals as perceived by national board(s) of safety; review of relevant research
- Lighted hallways throughout building
- Pinpointed access rooms to science equipment and chemicals
- Availability of fire extinguishers and clear, simple directions explaining how to operate them; location of alarms to activate in emergencies
- Periodic K-9 patrol of student lockers; classrooms and other areas as needed
- Student parking lot monitored for student activity and safety

Chapter Thirty-Nine

Old(er) Buildings Are Usually More Secure Than New Ones: They Were Built Better

Potential crisis: A security challenge?

In the first week of April—Wednesday, in fact—the school district board members, school safety teams, administrators, and a handful of faculty and staff members who could spare their time assembled at the high school gymnasium.

Each adult present had received a memo with check-off spaces and places for note-taking related to specific items, serving as an informal agenda for this school safety meeting. It was an early release day for students and most faculty members.

Athletic Director Bernie Clauser met the group at the locked door to the gymnasium; it seemed an odd place for a meeting. Clauser had received a note to meet with the safety group at this location.

Relevant background: The chief security officer, alert to any overlooked safety issues in the three unit district schools, had started a competition the second term of school called the Safety Challenge. Open to anyone, the contest asked school staff members in any capacity or any student of any grade level to suggest viable ideas to further increase the safety of any of the three school buildings. A good, workable safety suggestion merited a $25 award; an outstanding safety suggestion was worth a $50 award.

On that afternoon in April, Clauser opened the door and the group gathered inside the gym, and an instructor among those assembled switched on the lights.

A distant but distinct voice announced, "This is my safety suggestion." The voice came from the top balcony of the just-unlocked facility. It was Jonathan Daniels, a sophomore. He had somehow gotten into the gym. "Do I get the $50?" he yelled down to the group.

Security Chief Reynolds was the first to yell up to Daniels: "How did you get up there? And where did you get a key to this gym?" Clauser was already thinking about the write-up he would compose to penalize this usually well-mannered student who had no detentions or misbehaviors he knew about—up to this point, that is.

"I didn't use a key. I climbed the ceiling rafters, the walkway boards. You do know this gym connects to the rest of the high school, don't you?"

"No, Jon, I didn't know that," Reynolds replied.

"Yeah, it's true, but only at this height. I checked other possibilities already. Well, if I can climb those boards and just cut over here, anyone can." There was a pause. "That's a $50 safety idea, isn't it? I found an open area!"

The assembled adults looked at one another for a good, long minute. No one knew what to say. All manner of input, research, experts' advice, and people whose whole careers were spent in the building had apparently overlooked or did not know about this entry and connection. An individual had to be within the building to utilize the connection, but if students knew about it and wanted an escape route, this one was pretty unique. And the voice called again: "It's a $50 safety idea, isn't it?" Jon eagerly anticipated that money, no doubt about it.

"Doggone it, but you beat us," said Reynolds. "The $50 is yours." Turning to those assembled, he said, "We've got to close off this opening before someone else discovers it, if they haven't already." After a long silence, since no one among the group yet seemed to know what to say, he called up, "Can you get down safely or do you want us to come get you?"

"Sure. I'm coming down right now." And he turned and stepped, pirouetted, actually, like a well-practiced ballet dancer, retracing steps from an unknown entryway. In a manner of seven minutes or so, with the sound of steps and jumps only faint echoes, the student appeared, smiling, to his silent audience. A few looked with almost what appeared to be admiration at the sophomore.

Student input about many school issues, even safety concerns, is good, and student rewards may net useful input. Old school buildings may be a safe school's challenge—in some cases anyway.

About the Author

Helen M. Sharp is a freelance education writer, certified school administrator, and former educator. Her writings include more than fifty articles in state and national education publications, including *NASSP Bulletin* book reviews and two previous co-authored books: *The Educator's Writing Handbook* and *Case Studies for School Leaders: Implementing the ISLLC Standards*. She lives in Wake Forest, North Carolina, with two wonderful beagles and enjoys a part-time working schedule with the award-winning community newspaper *The Wake Weekly*. An avid fan of British procedurals, she corresponds with Roderic Jeffries, a prolific and renowned specialist of the genre. However, Sharp devotes as much time as possible to cooking, antiquing, exploring historic sites and keeping fit.